MW00777824

Nassau & Paradise Island, The Bahamas

Travel and Tourism

Author

Issac Harvey

Copyright Notice

Copyright © 2017 Global Print Digital
All Rights Reserved

Digital Management Copyright Notice. This Title is not in public domain, it is copyrighted to the original author, and being published by **Global Print Digital**. No other means of reproducing this title is accepted, and none of its content is editable, neither right to commercialize it is accepted, except with the consent of the author or authorized distributor. You must purchase this Title from a vendor who's right is given to sell it, other sources of purchase are not accepted, and accountable for an action against. We are happy that you understood, and being guided by these terms as you proceed. Thank you

First Printing: 2017.

ISBN: 978-1-912483-09-9

Publisher: Global Print Digital.
Arlington Row, Bibury, Cirencester GL7 5ND
Gloucester
United Kingdom.
Website: www.homeworkoffer.com

Table of Content

Introduction

A Paradise is found

Welcome to a fabled world that is full of life and free of cares. Nassau Paradise Island. A magical place that invites you to discover all things imaginative and inspiring, pulse-pounding and breathtaking, unbelievable and unforgettable. A mythical ocean paradise that once was lost, and now is found. Welcome to Atlantis, Paradise Island, Bahamas.

From the moment you arrive, you'll be immersed in a dazzling array of enchantments, luxuries, and pleasures. From one of the Caribbean's largest casinos to one-of-a-kind kid's adventures, world-class restaurant choices to impressive shopping, beaches and pools to the ultimate water experience, Aquaventure, Atlantis offers the perfect vacation in paradise. And you'll wonder how such a magnificent place exists...and how soon you can return. Prepare yourself for the most incredible vacation destination in the world. Prepare yourself for Atlantis.

History and Culture

Hidden among a group of islands poised between the Atlantic and Caribbean and only a few hundred miles from the United States' southern coast of Florida Nassau Paradise Island has sheltered everyone from pirates and freed slaves to blockade runners, rum smugglers and runaway lovers over the centuries. And although times are peaceful now, we still cherish a tradition of people making their own rules under sunny skies.

Gateway to the New World

The Bahamian island of Guanahani, traditionally identified as San Salvador, was Christopher Columbus' first landfall in the New World. The original inhabitants of the island were the Lucayans, described by Columbus as a peace-loving people, beautiful and generous of heart. Though Columbus claimed the island for Spain, the lack of gold here led the Spaniards to focus on settlements elsewhere in the Caribbean. In 1629, Charles I of England laid claim to the Carolinas and threw The

Bahamas in for good measure, a grand gesture that would weave together two of the major influences on The Bahamas' development England and the American South.

Spiritual Adventurers & Marauding Pirates

In 1648, William Sayles and his Eleutheran Adventurers (from the Greek word "Eleutheria" or "freedom") landed briefly in Nassau Harbour during their search for a place to establish a Puritan colony. They then sailed south to today's Eleuthera Island, where a reef called the Devil's Backbone wrecked the Adventurers' ship and chose their new home for them. The surviving Adventurers were the first English settlers in The Bahamas.

Back in Nassau (first established as Charles Town in 1666 and christened Nassau in 1695), wrecked ships became a livelihood for the city's less religious-minded settlers. If bad weather and poor maps didn't bring enough salvage ashore, the "citizens" of this outlaw settlement would put lights on the reefs to lure ships to their doom. Although the faraway English government did not approve of this rogue activity, they did put a seal of approval on the beginnings of piracy.

During the 17th century, England was constantly at war and the Royal Navy had its hands full, so a Letter of Marque was given to sea captains called "privateers", which allowed them to attack enemy ships. Piracy quickly became rampant, a "Privateer's Republic" was established in Nassau, and Edward Teach, better known as Blackbeard, declared himself Nassau's magistrate. Calico Jack Rackham, Anne Bonney and Mary Read were among many infamous pirates based here.

When England signed treaties with its enemies, the privateers (who had far exceeded the limits of their Letter of Marque) officially became outlaws. In 1718 their republic came to an end when England sent Governor Woodes Rogers to Nassau, armed with three warships and the motto Expulsis Piratis Resituta Commercia (Pirates Expelled Commerce Restored).

The Loyalists

The Bahamas then became an English royal colony and during the American Revolution many Loyalists fled here, some of them bringing slaves from plantations in the Carolinas. But plantations never became a successful way of life on the islands, and in 1807 when England's Parliament banned the slave trade the Royal Navy intercepted many slave ships bound for America and the captured West Africans were set free here. Nassau's Over-the-Hill district was first established as a settlement for liberated West Africans. By the time Parliament declared general Emancipation in 1834, about three-quarters of the Bahamian population was from West Africa.

During the American Civil War, privateering experienced something of a resurgence. England and Nassau defied the North's blockade and continued to trade with Southern states. In the famous Civil War novel Gone with the Wind, Rhett Butler is a well-known man about town in Nassau. Later, during Prohibition, Nassau defied the U.S. again and did a lively business smuggling liquor into Southern ports, until President Roosevelt repealed the "unfortunate amendment".

In the 1940s, King Edward VIII gave up his throne to marry "the woman I love" and settled in Nassau. The new couple, known as the Duke and Duchess of Windsor, began a new era of peaceful glamor here, attracting an ever-increasing number of visitors, celebrities and famous figures to our islands

Independence

In 1953, young politician Lynden Pindling, who had grown up in Nassau's West African Over-the-Hill district, formed the Progressive Liberal Party, which 20 years later led the nation to vote for independence from England. Our island still retains strong ties to England, choosing to remain within the Commonwealth and to declare allegiance to the Queen. At Nassau's Government House, official residence of the Governor-General, you can watch the Changing of the Guard twice a month or on the last Friday of each month, enjoy a traditional English Afternoon Tea with the Governor's wife.

Islands of Song

Musical traditions here reflect both the impact of history on the islands and a homegrown, distinctively national character. All through the islands of The Bahamas, music is woven deeply into the fabric of daily life so much so that one of the nicknames given to our archipelago is "the Islands of Song".

Blues and spirituals made their way down from the American South and took on a Bahamian flavor, in breezy seaside church choirs where rhyming spirituals are sung, and on homemade guitars in the hands of virtuoso performers like the legendary Joseph Spence and his contemporary Israel Forbes.

Junkanoo, goombay and rake 'n' scrape all incorporate the handclapping and drum rhythms of West African dance music. Goombay is a secular Bahamian tradition, danceable music full of stories about love and other daily dramas. Rake 'n' scrape bands are purely instrumental: a carpenter's saw, a goatskin drum and an accordion are all traditional rake 'n' scrape instruments. And the "gran' dance" of Junkanoo is, of course, the heart of our annual national celebration. Competing dance groups like the Valley Boys, the Music Makers and the Saxons Superstars spend all year creating fanciful costumes and practicing elaborate routines. If you can't be here for the holidays around Christmas and New Year's Day, a number of local venues feature Junkanoo performances or visit the Junkanoo Edu-Culture Museum.

True Bahamian

Given The Bahamas' historic and multicultural background, it's no wonder that Bahamian English is a fascinating mixture of Queen's diction, African influences and island lingo. Unfamiliar sounding words you'll hear on our streets and beaches may be survivors from early English settlement (true Shakespearean English), echoes of Africa or local slang. The "h" is often dropped in daily speech ('ouse for house or t'anks for thanks). You'll find conversation easy here. The distinctive sounds of daily speech are all part of a true Bahamian experience.

Travel and Tourism
Attractions on Paradise Island

Paradise Island is the type of place where you go for a luxury getaway and everything you could want or need is within reach. This includes entertainment and many activities to keep you busy, but, if this isn't enough for you, you may want to consider crossing the bridge back to the main section of New Providence Island (specifically Nassau) for cultural, historical, and natural attractions to explore.

Beaches

You will discover a large number of beaches to choose from on the island. Whether you're looking forward to people watching, or you prefer a quieter stretch of sand, you should find some appealing options. You can click on each beach name for a detailed guide to that section of the coast.

Paradise Beach: There are a number of small huts which provide a welcomed respite from the sun on this mile long strip of magnificent white powdery sand. The beach is considered one of the most beautiful beaches in all of the Bahamas, and the view at sunset will show you exactly why.

A second alternative to consider is Cabbage Beach. The most popular beach on Paradise Island, Cabbage Beach is a stunning strip of pearly white sand along the island's northern coast. Though consistently populated, this long beach has ample sand and sun for everyone. However, despite its popularity, there are no public restrooms so don't expect to be allowed the use of facilities unless you plan on having lunch at one of the hotels that line the beach.

Casuarina Beach: Once you arrive on Paradise Island from Nassau, head west passed Sunrise Beach Club and over the Paradise Beach Drive bridge. Follow Paradise Beach Drive until you reach Casuarina Beach.

The island has plenty of additional beaches. To reach our complete guide to beaches, read on Beaches page in this book.

Historical Sites

Do you like learning some of the history of countries you visit? If that's the case, you might enjoy visiting a historical site during your time on Paradise Island.

An interesting landmark worth visiting is Cloisters. It is found within eastern Paradise Island. The Cloisters are the ruins of a French Monastery with a lot of history. Built in the 1300's, the ruins did not find their way to the Bahamas until the 1960's.

Another common landmark for vacationers is The Caves. It is found in Cable Beach, West of Paradise Island. This easy to miss spot was once favored for its elusive nature -- it functioned as an ideal hideout for pirates that roamed the Bahamas and Caribbean Islands. As you explore this cave, it won't be hard to see why pirates chose this place for their home.

You can look through this table to see historic sites on and near the island.

HISTORIC SITES ON AND NEAR PARADISE ISLAND		
Name	Phone	Location
Cloisters	(242) 363-3000	3.9 mi. Northeast of Central Nassau
The Caves	(242) 302-2000	2.0 mi. West of Central Cable Beach

Miscellaneous Landmarks

Visitors can enjoy some other interesting landmarks on Paradise Island.

MISCELLANEOUS LANDMARKS ON PARADISE ISLAND			
Name	Type	Location	Island
Paradise Island Lighthouse	Lighthouse	0.9 mi. Northwest of Central downtown Nassau	New Providence

Parks and Botanical Gardens

Visitors can experience either of two parks, as well as a botanical garden on and near Paradise Island.

If you enjoy tropical vegetation, you might want to visit Versailles Garden, which is located in eastern Paradise Island. Versailles Gardens is located between the Ocean Club and Nassau Harbour.

The parks and gardens worth considering are displayed in the table below.

PARKS AND GARDENS ON AND NEAR PARADISE ISLAND		
Name	Type	Location
Atlantis Lagoon	Park	Central Paradise Island
Bonefish Pond National Park	Park	5.0 mi. South West of Central Nassau
Versailles Garden	Botanical Garden	3.9 mi. Northeast of Central Nassau

Zoos and Aquariums

If the idea of spending part of a day surrounded by sea life sounds like fun, consider visiting The Dig Aquarium. While "The Dig" may bring images of sand and dirt, that is not what you'll find here. The Dig at Atlantis is a stellar aquarium full of exotic exhibits themed to the sunk city of Atlantis.

AQUARIUMS ON PARADISE ISLAND			
Name	Type	Location	Island/th>
The Dig Aquarium	Aquarium	Central Paradise Island	New Providence

Land Formations

Another fun idea is to visit some of the more interesting naturally occurring land formations. Other types of natural attractions on Paradise Island are listed in the following chart.

LAND FORMATIONS ON PARADISE ISLAND		
Name	Type	Location
Atlantis Lagoons	Lagoon	Central Paradise Island
Paradise Lake	Lake	Central Paradise Island

Casinos

People don't generally stay on Paradise Island to gamble, but there is one such venue, Atlantis Casino. Stop by and try to win big at the Atlantis Casino. With nearly 1000 games going on at once, you can be sure there will be something for you, be it slots, or table games. There are even a few outdoor tables, letting you enjoy the weather, and hopefully a few wins.

Things to Do at Atlantis Paradise Island

Atlantis Paradise Island Resort is known worldwide for its amazing water adventures, white sand beaches, luxury accommodations and fine dining. Whether this resort on Nassau Paradise Island is on your bucket list or you're planning a return visit, your vacation days will be packed with fun with this list of top things to do at Atlantis Resort.

➢ Watch a complimentary movie in the Atlantis Movie Theatre. Located in the convention center rotunda, the Atlantis Movie Theatre offers Hollywood blockbuster movies and favorite movie-time snacks.

➢ Be on the lookout for special partnerships. When my daughter and I visited this summer, there was a Cartoon Network event going on that featured outdoor movies, parades, character meetings and a signature water obstacle course.

➤ Take a morning stroll along the shore to get the beach all to yourself. Whether you choose Cove Beach, Paradise Lagoon or Atlantis Beach, you'll find white-sand and gorgeous water views.

➤ Check out the shops and restaurants in Marina Village. Guests can peruse jewelry stores, clothing boutiques, restaurants and ice cream shops while enjoying local entertainers (and occasional parades) in a scenic waterfront setting.

➤ Take in a show with the Atlantis Live concert series. From Lady Gaga to Jerry Seinfeld, a wide range top performers are showcased throughout the year.

➤ Splurge for a private cabana rental. Whether you're traveling with a large family or with a spouse, a cabana offers pampering services, a private changing area, fans, fridge, exclusive pool access and electricity for all of your electronic devices (upgrades for WiFi too!).

➤ Dine like a local at Bimini Road in Atlantis Resort's Marina Village. Bahamian cuisine will please adults and kids alike at Bimini Road where guests can enjoy fresh seafood dishes, local favorites like Jerk chicken, conch stew and fritters, fried plantains and an extensive children's menu

➤ Indulge your sweet tooth at Carmine's. New York's famed Italian restaurant will please guests of all ages with pasta dishes and Italian specialties. If you've got a dessert lover in your group, the restaurant's Titanic dessert is not to be missed. (Think loads of ice cream and chocolaty cake!)

➤ Work off those vacation calories. Up to two guests per room, per day have complimentary access to the Fitness Center, including use of the cardio studio as well as universal and free weights.

➤ Take littlest travelers to Atlantis Pals where they can create their very own stuffed animals. Kids can choose from plush bears, dogs, cats and pink flamingos and outfit them with fun clothing and accessories.

➤ Step inside the the famous Atlantis Casino. Gamblers will be impressed by the Caribbean's largest casino where guests can play at more than 75 gaming tables. Non-gamblers will be wowed by the amazing Dale Chihuly glass sculptures. Need to improve your gaming skills? Check out the resort's daily complimentary gaming lessons.

➤ Snorkel the day away. Whether you bring your own gear or rent it at Atlantis, there are several great spots for snorkeling including Paradise Lagoon and Cove Beach. More adventurous water lovers can arrange for a snorkel boat trip or a snorkel outing to the Ruins Lagoon.

➤ Enjoy fine dining and celebrity chef inspired meals. Looking to celebrate a special occasion or just in the mood for a fabulous meal? Atlantis Resort's fine dining options range from traditional French to Asian fusion and everything in between including Nobu, Mesa Grill, Chop Stix, Olives and more.

➤ Explore the lost city of Atlantis' streets and tunnels at The Dig where kids and adults can explore dozens of marine life exhibits, sunken ruins and an interactive touch tank aquarium. Make sure to pick up a scavenger hunt map for the kids.

➤ Shop till you drop! Guests will find the worlds finest luxury stores (like Gucci, Versace, Michael Kors and David Yurman) as well as specialty stores (jewelry, fashion, beachwear, sporting goods, cigars, and more) and signature Atlantis souvenir gifts.

➤ Take the kids to Earth & Fire Pottery Studio where they can paint their own pottery. This shop features a wide selection of ready-to-paint ceramics and colorful glazes. If you're looking for an indoor activity, this is a great option.

➢ Get up close and personal with stingrays at Stingray Lagoon. Adults and kids will love watching these unique creatures swim in this shallow lagoon. Don't miss the chance to pet and feed them.

➢ Choose between lazy or wild river ride options. For a relaxing family-friendly float, the scenic Lazy River Ride will slowly transport you through a tropical landscape. For a more adventurous option, try out The Current which moves guests along via water escalators, rolling waves and extreme rapids.

➢ Spend the day at Aquaventure, Atlantis Paradise Island's 141-acre water park. From high-speed wateslides, river rides, kiddie splash areas and 11 pools, the largest water park in the Caribbean will entertain adults and children for hours and hours. (Note: Kids must be at least 48 inches tall to ride the slides.)

➢ Swim with dolphins at Dolphin Cay. Atlantis' Dolphin Cay is one of the largest and most sophisticated marine habitats in the world. For dophin lovers, the Shallow Water Interaction and Deep Water Swimencounters are a must.

Things to Do with Kids

Are you dreaming of a family vacation that will please foodies, shoppers, history buffs, animal lovers AND sun seekers? Nassau Paradise Island in the Bahamas is sure to please. If you're looking for fun activities beyond beach bumming, you'll love these five things to do on Nassau Paradise Island with kids.

1. Interact with dolphins and other marine life.

You don't need to be a guest at Atlantis Resort to interact with marine life on the hotel's grounds. Resort day passes can be purchased at the Discover Atlantis desk in Coral Towers for access to the resort's renowned water park and marine habitats. The Dig is where kids and adults get the chance to see hundreds of fish as they journey through the streets and tunnels of the fabled lost city of Atlantis. Kids will especially love the scavenger hunt maps and interactive touch tank aquarium filled with conchs, crabs and sea urchins.

At Dolphin Cay, pay to participate in a variety of memorable animal encounters during which you can kiss, hug and even swim with dolphins, sting rays and sea lions. My 5-year-old daughter and I loved the Shallow Water Interaction, a 30-minute in-water experience with dolphins that makes a great choice for first-timers and small children.

2. Soak up Bahamian history on Paradise Island.

Opened last year, the Heritage Museum of the Bahamas is jam-packed with kid friendly Bahamian artifacts ranging from prehistoric times to today. Families learn all about the history and heritage of the Bahamas including the days of Columbus, the piracy era, slavery and plantation life, the Maritimes of the 18th century, the days of the Duke of Windsor and current happenings. The museum's collection will fascinate kids of all ages with items such as a 4.5 billion year-old meteorite, historic toys, Junkanoo costumes, pirate memorabilia, and a replica of a general store. The museum is located on West Hill Street, walking distance from Bay Street

3. Experience the Golden Age of Piracy.

Nassau is known as the capital of piracy and the home of Blackbeard. If you've got a little pirate lover, the Pirates Museum of Nassau is a must visit. The Golden Age of Piracy lasted for thirty years (from 1690 to 1720) and Nassau was home to thousands of pirates during that time. Upon arrival at the Pirates Museum, you'll be greeted by a "real" pirate who will gladly pose for photos and welcome you inside. This interactive museum features exhibits like a moonlit dock where visitors will hear sounds of lapping water and see pirates celebrating at a nearby tavern. From there, guests board a replica of a pirate ship and learn about the lives and times of the pirate community. The exhibits are fairly dark and younger children may be scared of the wax figures (they are very real looking!) so plan accordingly. There is a well stocked gift shop and several fun photo-ops (guillotines anyone?) so plan to spend an hour checking it all out

4. Shop the Straw Market and Bay Street for Bahamian finds.

Nassau Paradise Island is a great spot for kids to buy some local specialties as souvenirs of their family vacation. In Nassau's famed Straw Market girls will go crazy for the handmade straw purses and tote bags featuring designs of their favorite princesses or characters (Elsa, Anna, Dora, Ariel, oh my...!). With hundreds of vendors you might feel overwhelmed so definitely take your time to decide what you want and be prepared to bargain for the best price.

Bay Street is the main drag of downtown Nassau. If you're in the market for jewelry or watches, you'll find a great selection of shops with duty-free prices. If you like rum cake, this is the place to try every variety. The best days to shop are when the cruise ships aren't in town so be sure to check with your hotel before heading out

5. Eat Caribbean cuisine like a local.

Exposing kids to local cuisine on vacation is a great way to encourage them to try different flavors and foods. The best spot for kids to explore Bahamian cuisine is Bimini Road in the Marina Village shopping district. Families can try local favorites like Jerk chicken, conch stew and fritters, fried plantains, and peas n' rice. For less adventurous eaters, a children's menu is available featuring pasta, breaded grouper fingers, chicken nuggets and other kid favorites served with veggie sticks and apple wedges.

Things to do in Nassau and Paradise

Deep historical character and beauty

Nassau, capital city of The Bahamas, lying on New Providence Island, the neighbour of Paradise Island, is both captivatingly old and new. This island pair maintains a distinct blend of international 21st century glamour, old-world charm and tropical ease, giving holidaymakers the freedom to do everything - or simply relax and do nothing at all on their visit to Nassau & Paradise Island.

Soak up the sights and sounds

Venture into the historic heart of Nassau, and you'll discover this thriving commercial centre retains pretty much all of its colonial heritage and appeal. You can admire the Georgian architecture, pastel-coloured wooden shops and offices scattered along lively Bay Street; hire a horse-drawn cart - called a surrey - and take a leisurely tour of old Nassau while your driver regales you with the local folklore.

Check out the numerous ancient sites, forts and the hand-carved Queen's Staircase with its awesome vistas of Nassau, Paradise Island & Bahamas views beyond.

Delve into Nassau's history and art

If you want to step back through the centuries in Nassau you can wander along to the Pompey Museum and take a good, long look at the display of artefacts, documents and drawings. For a more modern glimpse of Nassau & Paradise Island Bahamas art you won't want to miss the contemporary Bahamian art galleries and the cultural Junkanoo museum tour either.

Shopping and sporting in Nassau & Paradise Island

When you fancy getting active Nassau offers a plethora of sports to entertain the whole family - including golf, bahamas diving, tennis and squash. With duty free savings on famous brands passed on to shoppers in many stores, shopping in and around Nassau or Paradise Island is a delight. Souvenir hunters will enjoy the unique selection in the Straw Market; this is the one place on the island where you are free to haggle with the vendors - in fact, it's expected.

Where the action is...

From unmissable bargains to unforgettable beaches, take a walk along the fabulously colourful 'Bahamian Riviera', Cable Beach. Only three miles west of the city and easily accessible by bus or taxi, this magnificent stretch of exclusive resorts and homes on two and a half miles of golden sand is also the focus of Nassau & Paradise Island's Bahamas-style vibrant nightlife. Nightclubs, pubs, restaurants, and even a casino, are all just a short stroll away from each other.

Paradise Island Bahamas beauty at its best

Waiting to welcome you just a stone's throw from Nassau is the glamorous Paradise Island. Just six km long and 0.8 km wide, Nassau & Paradise Island are connected by two bridges. Looking at the beaches that curve along the north shore, the elegant resorts, or the championship level Cable Beach Golf Course, it's hard to believe that this was, until recently, an unused islet known as Hog Island. Things have certainly come a long way since those days on Paradise Island Bahamas visitors will find a lot to do.

World's largest open-air aquarium

Without doubt, the main attraction of Nassau & Paradise Island is the 14-acre Atlantis Waterscape, the world's largest open-air aquarium, which teems with over 100 species of colourful fish.

Paradise Island is also the drop-off point for the unforgettable Dolphin Encounter and the exhilarating Powerboat Adventures.

Giving shelter through the ages

Nassau's stunning natural harbour lies on the 33-km-long island of New Providence. Protected for a 4 km stretch by Paradise Island, this sheltered harbour has attracted settlers to Nassau and Paradise Island since long before the British colonists left Eleuthera and arrived in New Providence in the late 1600s

Family Fun

An affordable family vacation experience on Paradise Island

Comfort Suites Paradise Island is the perfect destination for your family vacation. There are activities and amenities that everyone in the family can enjoy from exploring historic sites in Downtown Nassau, to playing on the beach or rushing down the slides at Aquaventure.

With Comfort Suites you get the complete Nassau Paradise Island experience, with fun, sun and fine dining. The best part is that our affordable room rates and full access to Atlantis make it ideal for the whole family to stay and play.

Kids Stay, Play, And Eat Free

What makes Comfort Suites Paradise Island such an affordable family vacation destination in the Bahamas is its special offers. Check out our latest promotion where Kids can Stay, Play and Eat Free. Pair this offer with one of our latest airfare promotions and your choices for Bahamas Hotels just got a whole lot easier.

Atlantis Resort and Casino

When you stay at Comfort Suites Paradise Island, you have one of the biggest attractions in all of the Caribbean just steps away and best of all, as our guest you and your family will have complete access to all Atlantis facilities and amenities. Guests who stay at this Bahamas Hotel truly have the best of both worlds.

Dining Options
With 21 restaurants and 19 bars and lounges, dining options at the Atlantis cover the full range of culinary experiences. Bahamian food, Southwestern cuisine, buffets with regional options, steak, seafood and quick bites are available.

Attractions and Activities
The attractions at Atlantis make it one of the most unique & exciting destinations in the Caribbean. Aquaventure, a 141-acre water park has nine water slides, 11 pools, a mile-long tubing river, rock climbing, waterfalls, waters ports and a kids water-play fort. Atlantis location in

the Caribbean provides more traditional water adventures, such as snorkeling, scuba diving and scuba, a form of diving that does not require certification. Marine life is abundant. More than 108 million gallons of seawater flow through Dolphin Cay, several stocked lagoons, the Shark Lagoon, which can be experienced while riding through a clear tunnel water tube, and multiple aquariums, such as The Dig. Non-water activities include golf, tennis, pottery and a fitness center.

Shopping

Crystal Court Shops at Atlantis with names such as Gucci, Bulgari and Versace, to name a few, offer you hours of unparalleled shopping and indulgences. Designer fashions, souvenir boutiques, as well as jewelry and much more, will have you smiling as you shop til you drop.

Casino

The Temple of the Sun is the largest casino in the Bahamas. This Bahamas casino is open 24 hours a day and features 850 state-of-the-art slot machines and 90 table games, such as baccarat, blackjack, craps, roulette and Caribbean stud poker. The Pegasus Race and Sports Book offers wagering on all major sporting events, including US racetracks. Special events and tournaments are held in the casino such as a $50K Blackjack Tournament and a $75K Halloween Slot Tournament.

Nightlife

Nightlife entertainment includes the 9,000 square-foot Aura Night Club, the Atlantis Theater, which shows current Hollywood feature movies, and the Atlantis Live concert series highlighting artists such as Justin Beibre, Rihanna and Gloria Estefan. For a laugh, the Jokers Wild Comedy Club offers stand-up comedians from around the world performing Tuesdays through Sundays.

The Best Nightlife in the Bahamas

Staying at Comfort Suites Paradise Island is your ticket to after-dark fun and excitement. Begin the evening in one of the many Paradise Island restaurants. Make sure to pair your meal with a tasty tropical cocktail or some of the best wines in the world.

If you are up for some gambling, you will find the greatest gaming experience at Atlantis Casino. The Casino is the most artfully themed casino this side of Vegas and offers over 1,000 slot machines. Linger around one of the 90 table games and watch the sharks battle through a game of Blackjack or Texas Hold Em Poker. For more entertaining opportunities, Atlantis Casino also hosts many spectacular performances by chart-topping artists year-round.

If you want to relax with a cocktail after dinner, experience the sophisticated glamour of the Dune Bar at the One&Only Ocean Club. A free shuttle runs from the Coral Towers, and this service is offered to Comfort Suites guests as well.

If you want to party like a celebrity, head over to Aura Nightclub, inside the Casino and enjoy the beats spun by world-class DJs.

For a more relaxing island experience, stroll across the street to the Marina Village, an open-air marketplace, where you can visit shops, savor an ice-cream cone, browse boutiques, enjoy live music in front of Bimini Road, and gaze at the multi-million dollar yachts at dockside.

Beaches

Beaches on Paradise Island

From the "Average Joe" to the rich and the famous, people from all walks of life have been spotted on the dazzlingly white shores of Paradise Island. While those staying at the massive Atlantis Paradise Island Resort make up a good majority of the beachgoers, even tourists staying in Nassau and Cable Beach will make the drive over the bridge just to dip their toes in these bright blue waters.

Beach Choices in The Area

You will discover a large number of beaches to consider visiting on the island. Regardless of whether you enjoy people watching, or you'd rather find a more secluded spot, you should find some appealing options. To get full details a single beach simply click on the names of the ones you're curious about.

If you are wanting to snorkel, a location where that's an option is Casuarina Beach. Stunning pink sands and aquamarine waters typify Casuarina Beach. Just off shore is a patch of reef where visitors can swim with parrotfish and turtles.

Another place for beach-goers to consider is Pirates Cove Beach. You don't need to be hunting for buried treasure or wearing an eye patch to enjoy a day at Pirates Cove Beach. Instead, this is a popular spot on the small Staniel Cay for hiking and sunbathing.

Colonial Beach: A quieter area than some of the nearby beaches, Colonial Beach is a great spot catch some rays and watch the many boats coming in and out as they make their way around Paradise Island and into Nassau Harbor. There's also an interesting lighthouse - the Nassau Port Lighthouse - you'll want to check out a stone's thrown to the west.

Be sure to look through the table just below for more information about your options.

BEACHES ON PARADISE ISLAND		
Name	Location	Coast

Arawak Beach	3.1 mi. East of Central downtown Nassau	South East
Cabbage Beach	Central Paradise Island	South
Casuarina Beach	Central Paradise Island	North West
Colonial Beach	3.6 mi. North of Central Nassau	North East
Honeymoon Cove Beach	1.9 mi. East of Central Potters Cay	South East
Paradise Beach	Central Paradise Island	South West
Pirates Cove Beach	Central Paradise Island	South West
Snorkeler's Cove Beach	1.7 mi. East-Northeast of Central Potters Cay	South East

Fortunately, you'll be able to find additional types of attractions, read "Attraction page about other interesting attractions for Paradise Island.

Comfort Suites Paradise Island

When you arrive at Comfort Suites Paradise Island, you will be greeted by lush tropical foliage and beautiful palm trees. This affordable Bahamas Hotel is set within walking distance of a beautiful Paradise Beach, the perfect destination for your island vacation.

Dolphin Cay and Aquaventure

This tropical paradise features crystal clear, turquoise waters with average temperatures of about 80°F year-round. Add powder white sandy shores and you have a perfect sun tanning location. Enjoy the relaxing Bahamian breeze, wiggle your toes in the sand and then cool off with a refreshing dip in the ocean.

Atlantis features beautiful beaches, the Aquaventure water park, Dolphin Cay and so much more. Our guests have full use of facilities at Atlantis Resort and Casino. We're just steps away from all the fun and excitement.

Watersport activities on Paradise Island
Of course, there's more to do than basking in the suns glorious rays! Take the time to explore Paradise Island through exciting watersport activities. Join in a snorkeling adventure and discover colorful reefs and tropical fish. Take diving lessons and find out what its like to explore our Bahamian waters. Go fishing and experience the thrill of reeling in a big catch!

Shopping

Shopping in Nassau, Paradise Island
Welcome to the ultimate shoppers duty-free paradise! In January 1992, the Bahamian government took away the import duty on 11 categories of luxury goods, which means that you have the chance to save up to 35% on brand name items and bring back duty-free items up to a certain limit, without paying any additional taxes.

Marina Village in Atlantis
Marina Village in Atlantis is your source for luxury fashion, sports and beachwear. Explore the 21 shops in Marina Village that feature beautiful collections of the worlds finest timepieces and invigorating scents of brand name perfumes. Handmade Bahamian crafts, artwork and high-end jewelry can also be found here.

Crystal Court Shops at Atlantis
Crystal Court Shops at Atlantis with names such as Gucci, Bulgari and Versace, to name a few, offer you hours of unparalleled shopping and indulgences. Designer fashions, souvenir boutiques, as well as jewelry and much more, will have you smiling as you shop til you drop.

Across the bridge to Nassau, you can visit the Straw Market, the largest of its kind, for unique gift ideas such as straw baskets, mats, and hats. As you peruse through the outdoor Straw Market, you'll get a chance to learn more about Nassau and the Bahamian culture.

Paradise Island has it all, and no Bahamas Island shopping experience would be complete without visiting theParadise Island Straw Market.

Golf
Hit the Links at the Ocean Club Golf Course on Paradise Island

Challenge yourself on one of the Caribbeans most well manicured golf courses at Ocean Club Golf Course, located just minutes away at the One&Only Ocean Club Resort. Designed by Tom Weiskopt, the Ocean Clubs 18-hole championship golf course will give you a round of golf with breathtaking views. The fairways of this ocean front golf course in the Bahamas are lined with beautiful tropical foliage and offer spectacular views of both the Atlantic Ocean and Nassau Harbor.

Attracting every caliber of golfer, the par-72 course is known for its hole 17, which plays entirely along the scenic Snorkelers Cove. If you need pro advice on your game, consult with the Ocean Clubs on-site golf pro, Ernie Els, one of the top golf players in the world.

This premier Bahamas golf course is a vacation experience that every golfer should enjoy!

Ocean Club Golf Course
General Information

Green fees are $265.00* per 18 holes and include use of golf cart.
Rental Clubs and shoes are available.
Tee times can be booked on the day of play (if available).
Call 242-363-6682 for tee time availability

Attraction

Play at Paradise Islands Top Attractions like Aquaventure and Dolphins Cay at Atlantis

After enjoying your Complimentary Hot American Buffet Breakfast at Comfort Suites, set out to explore Nassau Paradise Island's most exciting attractions. With so many hotspots located just on one island, Comfort Suites isn't just a great Bahamas Hotel, it's a top Caribbean destination with vacation packages and unique experiences that the entire family can enjoy.

As a tropical mega resort, Atlantis Resort and Casino is often seen as the main attraction of Paradise Island. Influenced by the ruins of the Lost City of Atlantis, the resort will give you a holiday experience that you're unlikely to forget. Spend the day splashing around in the ocean, experience the thrilling water-slides of Aquaventure or swim with the dolphins at Dolphin Cay. Treat yourself and indulge in great cuisine at the many restaurants, or lounge by a pool with a tropical drink in hand. In the evening, join in the excitement of Atlantis Casino, Aura Nightclub or other bars and lounges.

Explore the history of Paradise Island
Explore the history of Paradise Island and take the time to visit the Cloisters, a 14th Century French stone monastery that was brought to Paradise Island brick by brick during the 1920s. You can enjoy the

leisurely 20-minute walk to this attraction, or hop on the Atlantis shuttle service and get dropped off just steps from the Cloisters. Another popular architectural attraction is the Queens Staircase, a 102-ft staircase which was carved out of coral-based sandstone by slaves in the 18th century. The staircase is located in Nassau, at the top of Elizabeth Street and near the Graycliff Hotel.

Nassau Straw Market

You don't always have to arrive on a cruise ship to visit a Bahamian Straw Market. The famous Nassau Straw Market is located in close proximity to Comfort Suites Paradise Island. Across the bridge to Nassau, you can visit the Straw Market, the largest of its kind, for unique gift ideas such as straw baskets, mats, and hats. As you peruse through the outdoor Straw Market, you will get a chance to learn more about Nassau and the Bahamian culture.

You can also take a short stroll towards the BahamaCraft Center, just a 2-minute walk away from Comfort Suites, and browse through a unique selection of arts and crafts. Find straw baskets, vibrant paintings and colorful Junkanoo masks that make for great souvenirs from your Paradise Island vacation.

Paradise Island Weddings

Plan your dream destination wedding with an experienced wedding planner

You have dreamt of this special day your entire life, an intimate destination wedding in Paradise Island on a white sandy beach with a romantic sun setting over a gentile turquoise ocean and your friends and family all there to witness a milestone moment.

Comfort Suites Paradise Island can recommend an experienced wedding planner to help with every detail for your big day. By choosing such a vibrant destination, your planner can suggest many venue options from the rehearsal dinner, to the ceremony and celebration. Your destination wedding will be executed flawlessly and she will assist in providing arrangements for all of your needs including family airport pick-ups, flowers, obtaining your license and booking the minister and event photographer.

Honeymoon Vacation

Spend less on the room rate and more on unique experiences for your Bahamas honeymoon vacation. Comfort Suites Paradise Island offers a romantic backdrop for your honeymoon with nearby beautiful beaches and the sizzling nightlife of Atlantis Resort and Casino all steps from your affordable Bahamas hotel junior suite.

Plan your dream honeymoon vacation on Paradise Island and you and your partner can indulge in the islands luxury spas, couture shopping and exquisite dining. Best of all, by planning your honeymoon vacation on Paradise Island you will be front and center to one of the worlds most extravagant Caribbean Destinations, Atlantis.

Dining on Paradise Island

Satisfy your appetite at Comfort Suites Paradise Island.
A dining experience on Paradise Island, Bahamas can be as captivating as a day spent on a white sandy beach. Spend your nights at Comfort Suites and you will have access to many restaurants that will allow you to sample delicious dishes from around the world. The convenient Comfort Suites Paradise Island location positions you within walking distance of many culinary delights found at Marina Village, Atlantis and other hot spots on Paradise Island.

Also for a limited time, kids who stay at this Paradise Island hotel also eat free at our on-site restaurant and many other restaurants nearby,

Restaurant & Lounges

Dining at Comfort Suites Paradise Island
Celebrity chef and fine dining, casual al fresco island meals, and quick-and-easy favorites: When it comes to delectable dining options in

delightfully different settings, Nassau Paradise Island is sure to satisfy every appetite and every palate, no matter what you crave. Enjoy an array of flavors ranging from classic French and family-style Italian to Asian-fusion and traditional Bahamian cuisine—a wonderful combination of Spanish, West African, and British influences.

Our Bahamas restaurants include casual beachfront cafés, celebrity chef restaurants, seaside bars and grills, familiar fast-food spots, and authentic Bahamian experiences like The Arawak Cay Fish Fry on West Bay Street just outside downtown Nassau. All are set against one of the most beautiful backdrops in the Caribbean.

From young and picky eaters to foodies exploring the latest culinary trends, the question will no longer be, "What's for dinner?" but "When can we come back again?"

Comfort Suites Paradise Island

Discover wonderful dining establishments, just steps from your Bahamas hotel room. Comfort Suites Paradise Island features an on-site restaurant open for breakfast and lunch, where you are sure to find something tasty to hit the spot when hunger strikes. Start your day with a delicious Complimentary Hot American Buffet Breakfast !

Complimentary Hot American Buffet Breakfast

The new Hot American Buffet Breakfast is full of hot and delicious options making breakfast at Comfort Suites hotels the perfect way to start your day. Enjoy our free, hot breakfast featuring eggs, meat, yogurt and fresh fruit, cereal and more...including your choice of hot waffle flavors! And if you are leaving early, a Your Suite Success&trade Grab & Go bag is available for the two hours prior to breakfast.

Breakfast Salon

Enjoy your Hot American Buffet Breakfast at our newly renovated Breakfast Salon.

Crusoe's Garden Restaurant

Enjoy casual indoor/outdoor dining at Crusoes Garden Restaurant located by our pool and browse through a lunch menu featuring burgers, sandwiches, salads and seafood. Open daily for breakfast, lunch, and dinner.

Crusoe's Pool and Swim-up Bar

If you truly cant bring yourself to leave the pool, simply swim-up to the poolside bar and enjoy a drink amidst a tropical setting and lush green foliage. The poolside bar is open daily from 11:00 a.m. to 7:00 p.m.

Bamboo Lounge

Wrap up a perfect tropical day at the Bamboo Lounge off the main lobby, and relax while sipping on your preferred Island drink. The

Bamboo Lounge is open daily from 4:00 p.m. until 11:30 p.m. Hours may vary. Check with front desk staff for updated hours.

Atlantis Restaurants & Lounges

Dine and Experience the world over at one of Atlantis' Restaurants

Step into a world of unique dining experiences. Explore Atlantis restaurants and sample some of the most delectable culinary dishes in the world. Your dining adventure will lead you to a variety of mouth-watering menu options, such as Italian, Japanese, Bahamian and more.

Marketplace, Royal Towers

The Marketplace provides a delightful Old World ambiance and a great variety of international foods. If you want a bit more than the Complimentary Hot American Buffet Breakfastat Comfort Suites, begin your day with an impressive breakfast buffet and later on, indulge in entrées that range from grilled burgers to seafood and pasta.

Mosaic, The Cove

The Mediterranean-influenced restaurant brings a fresh concept when it comes to custom-made cuisine. Mosaic prepares dishes on demand, from fresh fish to churrasco and is open daily for breakfast, lunch and dinner. A buffet is also featured.

Cave Grill

Grab a quick burger or hot dog in a Bahamian cave and experience close-up underwater views of a thriving habitat.

Seagrapes

Fun family favorites with an Island splash! Watch entrees come to life at our live-action cooking stations and enjoy the relaxed atmosphere in this fun dining room. Overflowing with culinary delights from around the world, including our BBQ smoke station and delightful Caribbean touches.

Shark Bites

Located at the base of the Mayan Temple, this Bahamian/deep sea fishing themed fast food restaurant and bar serves fresh Bahamian and Caribbean dishes with live Bahamian music.

Lagoon Bar and Grill, Coral Towers

Lunch at the Lagoon Bar and Grill gives you a chance to enjoy fresh salads and sandwiches on the open-air terrace while watching the sharks swim by.

Atlas Bar and Grill

The Atlas Bar and Grills 150 signature and specialty drinks and its 40 types of beef, chicken, veggie and seafood burgers definitely gives you the dining experience of a lifetime.

Bahamian Club, Coral Towers

Perfect for traditional fine dining, a culinary experience at the Bahamian Club begins with gourmet salads, followed by the finest cuts of steak, including Chateaubriand for two.

Café at the Great Hall of Waters, Royal Towers

Delight yourself in the Cafes exquisite menu selection as rainbow-hued fish float past huge plate-glass windows that illuminate the underwater ruins of Atlantis. A la carte items during breakfast and continental dishes for lunch are available to enjoy.

Casa D'Angelo, Coral Towers

The Islands best Italian cuisine is shown through Chef Angelo Elias culinary talents. Casa DAngelos menu includes homemade soups, fresh salads and a variety of pasta dishes.

Chopstix

Indulge in Chopstixs traditional Chinese recipes such as wok-fried grouper filets, sweet and sour chicken and sautéed sliced beef where the freshest and highest quality ingredients are always used.

Mesa Grill, The Cove

Southwestern style cuisine and vibrant Bahamian spices are the highlights of the Mesa Grill. Sink your teeth into specialties designed by renowned Chef Bobby Flay and enjoy breathtaking views of Atlantis from any seat in the Mesa Grill.

Nobu

Experience a new trend in Japanese cuisine from celebrated Japanese chef Nobu Matsuhisa. Savor favorites that include new style sashimi.

Marina Village Restaurants

Take a short stroll across the street to Marina Village and you'll find yourself surrounded by a variety of dining options. From traditional Bahamian dishes to gourmet cuisine, the restaurants at Marina Village will only leave you hungry for more. There is no shortage of great Restaurants at Marina Village on Paradise Island.

Cleito's Cart

Enjoy a quick lunch on the patio, or take it to go. Selections include hot Panini sandwiches, fruit and green salads.

Dive Inn

Sink your teeth into tantalizing barbeque items dipped in a smoky molasses barbeque sauce and a blend of exotic local herbs and spices. Taste local favorites that include native conch fritters and island-spiced pumpkin pie.

Jamba Juice

Get an extra boost of energy for your Island adventure with a nutritious fruit-filled smoothie, made fresh and full of vitamins and minerals.

Marina Pizzeria

Enjoy a traditional pizza with the toppings of your choice on the outdoor terrace overlooking the yachts in the Marina.

Murray's Deli

Grab a bite to eat at this New York style deli and enjoy the views of the Marina. Why not drop by for a hot pastrami or corned beef sandwich for lunch or dinner?

Johnny Rocket's

All-American favorites are available at Johnny Rockets family restaurant. Enjoy a juicy hamburger and shake in a fun 1950s style diner.

Pisces

Traditional Bahamian conch salad, batter-fried fish and chips, conch fritters, sandwiches, fresh fruit and refreshing drinks are available to go.

Tortuga Rum Cake Factory

Take a bite out of a homemade Bahamian rum cake or take one home as a souvenir. They come in a variety of flavors, such as banana, coconut, key lime and pineapple.

Village Creamery

Nothing cools off a hot day better than a visit to this ultimate ice-cream parlor. Choose from a variety of Haagen-Dazs favorites, including hand-dipped cones, milkshakes, floats, and sorbets.

Bimini Road

Get a taste of Island culture with Caribbean fare and colorful Junkanoo decor. The grand open kitchen features a one-of-a-kind conch station where fresh, Bahamian conch is prepared to order. Check out the live entertainment outside, too.

Carmine's

Enjoy classic Italian meals in a lively atmosphere. The meals at this famous New York landmark are served in generous portions so you can share with family and friends.

Café Martinique

Indulge in the gourmet cuisine of famed chef Jean-Georges Vongerichten. Café Martinique provides a unique dining experience with the melodious sounds of a Steinway piano and a spectacular marina view.

Seafire Steakhouse

Sumptuous meals full of rich, smoke, seared and grilled flavors are the highlight of your dining experience at the Seafire Steakhouse. Find the perfect wine to complement your meal, or choose from a variety of signature drinks.

Starbucks

Get your caffeine fix in Paradise Island and start the day with a delicious signature drink, hot or cold. Take a coffee break and enjoy the views of the marina.

More Paradise Island Restaurants

Step into a world of unique dining experiences. In addition to Atlantis' restaurants, explore some nearby Paradise Island favorites with a variety of mouth-watering menu options.

Anthonys Caribbean Grill at Paradise Village

Discover an assortment of creative and traditional Caribbean and American cuisine at this family friendly restaurant. Located in the heart of Paradise Island, across the street from Comfort Suites,

Anthonys Caribbean Grill varied menu makes the restaurant a popular spot to eat.

Columbus Tavern at Paradise Harbour Club

The only native waterfront restaurant overlooking the Nassau Harbor, Columbus Tavern provides the best of Bahamian and International cuisine with meals like conch fritters and mouth-watering guava.

Clubhouse at The One and Only Ocean Club

The Clubhouse overlooks the 9th and 18th holes of the spectacular Ocean Club Golf Course, and provides a perfect location for a light lunch. After a round of golf, catch up on the latest sports news at the Clubhouses full service bar.

Dune at the One and Only Ocean Club

Internationally renowned chef and restaurateur Jean-Georges Vongerichten brings his culinary talents to Dune. Prepare for a dining experience unlike any other with dishes featuring French-Asian cuisine with a touch of Bahamian influences.

Nassau Tour

Shallow-Water Dolphin Swim

Stand in the water alongside playful dolphins as you watch them swim back and forth in a beautiful lagoon. Learn about these incredible creatures as you get close enough to touch them, witnessing their incredible abilities as you view them swimming underwater at fantastic speeds.

Before you get into the water, listen to an informative briefing in the orientation theater, where a Marine Mammal Specialist provides an animated presentation on dolphin behavior and physiology. Then it's time to head to one of 3 lagoons, where you can climb into the waist-deep water to get up close to these amazing Atlantic bottlenose dolphins.

Feel free to touch the dolphins when they swim up beside you, and go underwater with a facemask to watch their astounding swimming abilities. Throughout your experience, a personal photographer is snapping photos to ensure you have keepsake candid shots to remember this experience. Afterwards, enjoy all-day access to Dolphin Cay's luxurious beach

Highlights
- ➢ Up-close encounter with playful Atlantic bottlenose dolphins
- ➢ Knowledgeable dolphin trainer provides fascinating insight
- ➢ Private access to the resort's secluded white-sand beach
- ➢ Chance to learn about marine rescue efforts at Dolphin Cay
- ➢ Underwater viewing of dolphin's incredible swimming tricks

Inclusions

➢ Shallow-water swim experience at Dolphin Cay

➢ Admission to Dolphin Cay's private beach

➢ Orientation

➢ Snorkel, mask, and souvenir bag

➢ Use of wetsuits, towels, lockers, and showers

➢ Non-alcoholic beverages

Exclusions

➢ Photos available for purchase

Know Before You Book

➢ Children 3 and younger are complimentary when accompanied by a paying adult.

➢ Children 10 and younger must be accompanied by a paying adult.

➢ Participants with special needs or physical impairments must have a primary attendant present throughout the interaction.

➢ Commentary is in English only. Guests must understand English or have a translator present at all times.

➢ In the event of inclement weather as defined by Dolphin Cay, programs will be rescheduled without penalty.

➢ Maximum group size is 6 people.

➢ Check-in is 15 minutes prior to the booked activity start time.

Cancellation Policy: This reservation is non-refundable and cannot be changed or cancelled after booking.

Location: Dolphin Cay at Atlantis, One Casino Drive West, Nassau, Bahamas

Exuma Islands Powerboat Adventure

Hop aboard a high-speed powerboat and jet across the waves to the serene and stunning Exuma Cays. Encounter the endangered Bahamian dragon, feed stingrays and sharks, kick back on a pristine beach, and enjoy a delicious waterfront lunch with an open bar during your day on this secluded isle.

Grab a seat in the back of a speedboat and skim over the sea at a thrilling 40 mph (65 kph) to Allen Cay. Here, meet the critically endangered Bahamian Dragon. You have a chance to observe and even feed grapes to the ancient and rare Allen Cay Rock Iguana.

From there, climb back into the boat and speed off to Ship Channel Cay, your private island for the day. Enjoy snacks and refreshments, stroll the scenic 2.5-mile (4-km) length of the island, go for a dip in the turquoise waters, or lounge in the shade of a beachfront fishing cottage.

Grab a drink from the open bar as your friendly crew starts grilling fresh fish for your lunch. You're not the only ones who are hungry on the island, though graceful stingrays and even fearsome sharks all cozy up to shore for a snack at feeding time. Watch this incredible marine spectacle as you fill your plate with savory island dishes.

The rest of the afternoon is yours for swimming, snorkeling, and relaxing on the white-sand beach with a drink in hand before the 1-hour boat ride back to Nassau

Highlights
➢ Thrilling high-speed powerboat ride to secluded Exuma Cays

➢ Encounters with rare Bahamian dragons, stingrays & sharks

➢ Delicious beachside lunch of fresh island-style specialties

➢ Open bar with tropical cocktails & unlimited refreshments

➢ Pristine beaches & crystal waters for swimming & snorkeling

Inclusions
➢ Guided snorkeling tour

➢ Powerboat ride from Nassau to the Exuma Cays

➢ Snorkel equipment & instruction

➢ Lunch

➢ Open bar

➢ Roundtrip transportation to and from select Nassau Hotels

Know Before You Book
➢ Children 2 and younger are not allowed.

➢ If you have back problems, broken bones, or a heart condition, you may not take part.

➢ If you are pregnant, you may not take part.

Cancellation Policy: You can cancel free of charge until 72 hours before your reservation starts. After that time, no cancellations, changes or refunds will be made.

Location: Exuma Island, Exuma Bahamas

Funky Nassau Half-Day Tour with Lunch & Local Drinks

See Nassau with fresh eyes during a guided sightseeing experience in a custom Jeep Wrangler. With the gentle sea breezes wafting in through the windows, travel to iconoclastic galleries, legendary forts, natural caves, and a fish fry where you can sample local treats with unlimited soft drinks.

Your tour begins with convenient hotel pickup and a pleasant cruise along the waterfront. Breathe the salty ocean air tinged with light floral notes and feel the sunlight kissing your skin. Stop at the center where outfits for the annual Junkanoo parade are prepared and marvel at the neon costumes that figure prominently in the celebration, and then venture to the Bahamas National Trust Retreat for a stroll through the region's flourishing greenery.

As you continue on your way, make additional stops at a traditional tea house, a gallery showcasing artisan wares, and John Watling's Distillery, where you can taste a signature pale, amber, or reddish-gold rum. Your tour isn't complete without a look at a series of military forts and limestone caves. During the journey, use your personal touchscreen to soak up additional information about historic Nassau.

When your stomach starts to rumble, head to the Arawak Cay Fish Fry, which some have likened to a state fair. Stroll between the food stalls, and then sit down to a delicious meal composed of fresh fish, conch salad, and soft drinks. If you like, purchase a beer produced by a local microbrewery and toast to your unforgettable adventures

Highlights
- ➢ Premier sightseeing tour to unlock the charms of Nassau
- ➢ The best of the Bahamas in a customized Jeep Wrangler
- ➢ Personal touchscreen & engaging videos for bonus info
- ➢ Visits to galleries, forts, natural caves & a rum distillery
- ➢ Tasty lunch with a fish fry and unlimited local sodas

Inclusions

- ➢ Guided tour of Nassau in a Jeep Wrangler

- ➢ Admission fees

- ➢ Lunch and unlimited local soft drinks

- ➢ Roundtrip transportation to and from the Nassau Bahamas Cruise Terminal and select Paradise Island and downtown Nassau hotels

- ➢ Live tour commentary provided in English

Exclusions

- ➢ Local beer

Know Before You Book

- ➢ Children 6 and younger are not allowed.

- ➢ You must be 18 years of age and present a valid photo ID in order to consume alcohol.

- ➢ This activity is not wheelchair accessible.

- ➢ Tour stops vary.

- ➢ Roundtrip transportation is available from the Nassau Bahamas Cruise Terminal, and from select hotels in Paradise Island and Downtown Nassau. Please arrange pickup from your hotel or a nearby location when you call to confirm your reservation.

➢ Pickups take place beginning 1 hour before your scheduled tour start time, depending on your hotel's location. You will receive confirmation of your exact tour departure time when you call to confirm your reservation.

➢ Please be ready and waiting in your hotel lobby 15 minutes prior to your scheduled pick-up time.

Cancellation Policy: You can cancel free of charge until 72 hours before your reservation starts. After that time, no cancellations, changes or refunds will be made.

Location: Multiple Locations Visited, Nassau, New Providence Bahamas

Deep Water Dolphin Swim

Dive into the deep waters of Dolphin Cay and emerge with incredible photos of your interaction experience. Get familiar with the fascinating behavior of dolphins possibly the smartest mammals on earth as you join their aquatic dance and even get the chance to feed, hug, and kiss them.

Meet the dolphin experts in the orientation room and begin to learn about dolphin behavior, physiology, and the importance of conservation during an animated presentation. Learn the safety information for interaction and get suited up for your dolphin deep dive.

Relish the opportunity to get up close and personal with these beautiful and intelligent mammals, marveling at the subtleties of their movements and mannerisms. Get a chance to feed, hug, and kiss the dolphins in the beautiful waters, and even get "foot pushed" by dolphins as they propel you across the lagoon. After your unforgettable swim, enjoy day-long access to the private beach to end your experience.

Highlights
➢ Up-close encounter with playful Atlantic bottlenose dolphins

➢ Beautiful swimming in dolphin pool with amazing foot push

➢ Knowledgeable trainer provides training information & tricks

➢ Private access to the resort's secluded white-sand beach

➢ Chance to learn about marine rescue efforts at Dolphin Cay

Inclusions
➢ Deep water dolphin swim at Dolphin Cay

➢ Admission to private beach

➢ Orientation

➢ Souvenir snorkel, mask, and bag

➤ Use of wetsuits, towels, lockers, and showers

➤ Non-alcoholic beverages

Exclusions
➤ Photos available for purchase

Know Before You Book
➤ Children 5 and younger are not allowed.

➤ Children 13 and younger must be accompanied by a paying adult.

➤ Children ages 6–9 must wear a life preserver.

➤ If you are pregnant, you may not take part.

➤ Participants with special needs or physical impairments must have a primary attendant present throughout the interaction.

➤ Commentary is in English only. Guests must understand English or have a translator present at all times.

➤ In the event of inclement weather, programs will be rescheduled without penalty.

➤ Maximum group size is 6 people.

➤ Check-in is 15 minutes prior to the booked activity start time.

Cancellation Policy: This reservation is non-refundable and cannot be changed or cancelled after booking.

Location: Dolphin Cay at Atlantis, One Casino Drive West, Nassau, Grand Bahama Bahamas

Blue Lagoon Dolphin Swim

Swim and play with dolphins and even get the opportunity to hug and dance with these gentle marine animals. Experience the thrill of dolphins propelling you across a lagoon and learn about these playful animals, training techniques, and ocean conservation.

After a 20-minute ride in a catamaran from Nassau, reach Blue Lagoon Beach. Enjoy playful and educational interaction with dolphins in the turquoise waters of the natural ocean lagoon. Your program begins with an orientation, brief commentary about the natural history of dolphins, animal training techniques, and ocean conservation, as well as Watchable Wildlife Guidelines.

Once in your life jacket, experience the joy of a dolphin kiss and a hug. Dance with these wonderful animals and marvel at their strength as you are propelled across the lagoon in the finale the footpush. In this program, trainers focus on allowing everyone to have quality time with the dolphins. Your excursion also includes access to the Aqua and Tropical Paradise Bounce Inflatable Parks

Highlights

- Opportunity to get up close & personal with playful dolphins

- Chance to swim, touch & play with gentle marine mammals

- Scenic & comfortable 20-minute catamaran ride from Nassau

- Access to Aqua & Tropical Paradise Bounce Inflatable Parks

Inclusions
- Admission to Blue Lagoon Beach

- Dolphin swim program

- Admission to Aqua and Tropical Paradise Bounce Inflatable Parks

- Lifejacket and wetsuit

- Use of hammocks, picnic tables, play areas, and water toys

- Use of lockers, changing areas, and showers

- Roundtrip transportation to and from Nassau via catamaran

Exclusions
- Premium water sports, including kayak rentals, water bikes, and underwater scooters

- Additional beverages from the Tropical Beach Bar

- Transportation to and from your hotel

Know Before You Book
- You must be 6 or older to participate in the Dolphin Swim.

- Children 12 and younger must be accompanied by a paying adult.

➢ If you are pregnant, you may not take part.

➢ Check-in is 30 minutes prior to the booked tour start time.

Cancellation Policy: You can cancel free of charge until 72 hours before your reservation starts. After that time, no cancellations, changes or refunds will be made.

Location: Blue Lagoon Island, Blue Lagoon Island, Bahamas

Ultimate Watersports Package

Experience the best of the Bahamas coast with a combination of thrills in, on, and above the water. This package takes you parasailing and snorkeling, gives you a ride on a jet ski and banana boat, and features plenty of time for you to admire the sights.

It starts with an easy pickup from your hotel or Nassau's cruise port, bringing you straight to the beach. Here, you get a quick introduction to the watersports on offer before you set out to enjoy your time on the coast.

First, climb aboard a jet ski to rocket out across the water and feel the thrill of the high-powered craft. Once you've tried splashing over the tropical waters, gear up for a few minutes spent parasailing as a motorboat and parachute help to raise you above the waters of Cabbage Beach for a spectacular view of the island.

Next, a banana boat carries you for a ride that along 3.5 miles (5.5 km) of warm Bahamian waters, so hold on and admire the sights on a perfect adventure to share with your family or friends. The experience wraps up with an hour spent snorkeling at a local reef, where you can see the lively tropical fish teeming below the surface of the sea. Wrap up the experience with an easy ride that takes you back to your hotel or cruise ship, where you can plan your next adventure.

Highlights
- ➤ Jet ski ride in the warm, gorgeous Caribbean waters
- ➤ Bird's-eye views of the beach & ocean while parsailing
- ➤ Exciting banana boat ride in the warm Caribbean waters
- ➤ Time for snorkeling among coral reefs & tropical fish
- ➤ Beautiful views of Cabbage Beach & Paradise Island

Inclusions
- ➤ 15-minute banana boat ride
- ➤ 15-minute jet ski ride
- ➤ Parasailing experience
- ➤ Snorkel, mask, and fin rental

➢ Life jacket

➢ Roundtrip transportation to and from most central Nassau hotels or the Nassau cruise port

Know Before You Book

➢ Children 4 and younger are not allowed.

➢ You must be at least 48 inches (122 cm) tall.

➢ You must weigh less than 300 pounds (136 kg). For solo parasailing, you must weigh at least 50 pounds (23 kg).

➢ You must be 16 or older to drive a jet ski.

➢ If you are pregnant, you should not take part.

➢ Flotation devices are available.

➢ If you have limited mobility, you should not take part.

➢ Hotel pickup is available from most centrally located Nassau hotels and the Nassau cruise port. Please arrange pickup from your hotel or a nearby location when you call to confirm your reservation.

➢ You will receive confirmation of your exact tour departure time when you call to confirm your reservation.

Cancellation Policy: You can cancel free of charge until 72 hours before your reservation starts. After that time, no cancellations, changes or refunds will be made.

Location: Cabbage Beach, Paradise Island, Bahamas

Parasailing Adventure from Cabbage Beach

Take to the skies high above the crystal-clear blue waters of Cabbage Beach on this exhilarating parasailing adventure. Soak up the sunshine as you're treated to epic views of The Bahama's gorgeous beaches while flying alongside the tropical coast.

Your journey begins when you're picked up at your hotel or cruise ship terminal, your guide transporting you to Cabbage Beach on stunning Paradise Island. Cross over the magnificent white-sanded shores as you board a speed boat that takes you out to the glittering ocean waters. Prepare for your exciting ride as your guide straps you into a safety harness before the boat takes off, the sail inflating as you are pulled up from the boat, beginning your flight above.

Glide through the air as you gain altitude, enjoying breathtaking views of the beach from this heightened altitude. Take in the sight of tropical forests, stunning beaches, and the turquoise sea beneath you. As your flight comes to an end, your guide gently pulls you back into the boat.

After your ride, feel free to spend the remainder of your day swimming in the water or relaxing on the beach.

Highlights

➢ Birds-eye views of the beach & ocean while parsailing

➢ Beautiful Cabbage Beach on Paradise Island's shores

➢ Choose from single or double rider parasailing experience

➢ Small group ensures personal service & instruction

➢ Opportunity to relax on the beach after your exciting ride

Inclusions

➢ Parasailing

➢ Life jacket

➢ Roundtrip transportation to and from your Nassau hotel or cruise port

Know Before You Book

➢ Children 4 and younger are not allowed.

➢ You must be at least 48-inches (122-cm) tall.

➢ You must weigh less than 350 pounds (159 kg).

➢ To fly solo you must weigh at least 50 pounds (23 kg).

➤ If you are pregnant, you should not take part.

➤ Flotation devices are available.

➤ If you have limited mobility, you should not take part.

➤ Hotel pickup is available from most centrally located Nassau hotels and the Nassau cruise port. Please arrange pickup from your hotel or a nearby location when you call to confirm your reservation.

➤ You will receive confirmation of your exact tour departure time when you call to confirm your reservation.

Cancellation Policy: You can cancel free of charge until 72 hours before your reservation starts. After that time, no cancellations, changes or refunds will be made.

Location: Cabbage Beach, Paradise Island, Bahamas

VIP Beach Experience on Blue Lagoon Island

Live like a true celebrity with the VIP Beach Experience in the spectacular surroundings of Blue Lagoon Island. A scenic boat ride carries you out to the tiny Atlantic island, where you can relax on a private beach with the beautiful sights and exquisite service to create a memorable stay.

A catamaran cruise carries you from Nassau's historic harbor, past its lush landscape of coconut trees, and onto the vividly turquoise waters from which Blue Lagoon Island gets its name. When you step ashore, you're escorted to a private coconut grove for some time to relax with a champagne mimosa in the calm, shady garden before you step onto the beach.

Your VIP area on the waterfront offers you comforts like ice tea, lemonade, seasonal fruits and vegetables, and entrées like grilled fish and chicken served buffet-style beneath the coconut palms. You can relax in the large double hammocks set up along the shore, have some fun in the Aqua bounce park, see the dolphins and sea lions in the marine habitats, or just go for a stroll along the spectacular lagoon.

With plenty more to do in the island's public areas and just off the shores, your hosts can help you arrange your ideal day. Make sure you get your own authentic Bahamian experience before the time comes for your cruise back to Nassau

Highlights
> Free time to relax on the sand & swim in the turquoise water

> Scenic & comfortable 30-minute catamaran ride from Nassau

> Greetings with a refreshing towel & champagne mimosa

> Access to Aqua & Tropical Paradise Bounce Inflatable Parks

➢ Chance to play volleyball, soccer, ping pong & board games

Inclusions
➢ Admission to the VIP Beach area at Blue Lagoon Beach

➢ Welcome drink, water, ice tea and lemonade

➢ Buffet lunch

➢ Use of lockers, changing areas, and showers

➢ Roundtrip transportation to and from Nassau via catamaran

Exclusions
➢ Kayak rentals, water bikes, paddleboards, and underwater scooters

➢ Animal encounters

➢ Additional beverages not listed as Inclusions

Know Before You Book
➢ You must be 21 or older.

➢ This activity is not wheelchair accessible.

➢ Maximum group size is 40 people.

➢ Check-in is 30 minutes prior to the booked tour start time.

Cancellation Policy: You can cancel free of charge until 72 hours before your reservation starts. After that time, no cancellations, changes or refunds will be made.

Location: Blue Lagoon Island, Bahamas

Blue Lagoon Beach Day

Just a short catamaran cruise from Nassau, Blue Lagoon Island is home to tropical birds and colorful aquatic life. Swim in the calm lagoon, float on Big Boss noodles and beach inner tubes, and relax on the white-sand beach.

After a 20-minute catamaran cruise, arrive at Blue Island Lagoon and spend the day on the white-sand beach. Enjoy water sports, a grilled lunch, and refreshing drinks or just relax and watch the coconut palms sway while you lounge in a hammock.

At your leisure enjoy a game of volleyball, soccer, or ping pong or play board games and take a dip in the beautiful lagoon. Get a chance to float on Big Boss noodles and inner tubes and enjoy access to Aqua Inflatable Park. If you like, you can rent kayaks or water bikes or go snorkeling for an extra fee.

Whether you want to lounge in a hammock, swim in the turquoise water of the lagoon, enjoy land and water sports, or purchase a refreshing cocktail at the Tropical Lagoon Bar, this excursion offers plenty of activities for the whole family

Highlights

- ➢ Free time to relax on the sand & swim in the turquoise water

- ➢ Scenic & comfortable 20-minute catamaran ride from Nassau

- ➢ Access to Inflatable Aqua Park

- ➢ Chance to play volleyball, soccer, ping pong & board games

- ➢ Breathtaking beaches with hammocks, beach chairs & picnic tables

Inclusions

- ➢ Admission to Blue Lagoon Beach

- ➢ Use of hammocks, picnic tables, play areas, and water toys

- ➢ Use of lockers, changing areas, and showers

- ➢ Roundtrip transportation to and from Nassau via catamaran

- ➢ Buffet lunch with fruit punch, iced tea, or lemonade

Exclusions

- ➢ Kayak rentals, water bikes, paddleboards, and underwater scooters

- ➢ Additional beverages

Know Before You Book

- ➢ Children 3 years and younger are complimentary.

- ➢ Children 12 and younger must be accompanied by a paying adult.

- ➢ Check-in is 30 minutes prior to the booked tour start time.

Cancellation Policy: You can cancel free of charge until 72 hours before your reservation starts. After that time, no cancellations, changes or refunds will be made.

Location: Paradise Island Ferry Terminal, 1 Marina Drive, Paradise Island, Nassau Bahamas

More Vacation Activities

Activities on Paradise Island
The quintessential tropical tourist destination, Paradise Island is home to one of the most popular resorts in the Caribbean, and from the pristine beaches to the spectacular nightlife, every activity caters to the needs of visitors from around the world.

Any and every activity you could imagine wanting to do here is available with ease. The Atlantis Resort, which accounts for more than 10 percent of the Bahamas GDP, has a water park, golf course tennis clubs, shopping, several pools, a casino, and a spa. Over the rest of the island you'll find another golf course, a comedy club, dolphin encounters, a lagoon, and plenty of shopping.

All of the Caribbean's favored watersports are available here as well, including snorkeling, scuba diving, sailing, and fishing.

Diving

Paradise Island, more or less, is one big aquatic themed resort. Part of this involves plenty of options for divers looking to explore the seas of the Bahamas.

There are two dive services and at least 6 different dive sites in the area. Readers can obtain more information concerning diving opportunities in this area, can do so on Diving page in this book.

Golf

Like to golf? There are a couple of golf courses in the area. The area courses are Paradise Island Golf Courseand Royal Blue. Click on the name of the course to read a detailed article concerning the course, including location, number of holes, and more. Follow this link to view our discussion of golfing throughout the Bahamas.

Sailing and Boating

The table right below summarizes some key facts concerning area firms that will enable you to spend some time out on the open water.

BOATING OPPORTUNITIES ON PARADISE ISLAND				
Name	Type	Phone	Location	Island
Flying Cloud	Boating and Day-Sailing Provider	(242) 394-5067	1.3 mi. East of Central downtown Nassau	New Providence

If you want to read about local marinas and charter options, see Sailing & Boating page in this book.

Shopping

If you have some shopping aficionados in your group, they can explore some of the 28 retail shops in the area. You can go to Shopping page in this book if you'd like to find out more about shopping both on Paradise Island and in nearby areas.

Sightseeing

Yet another great activity for visitors is to discover the area's sights and natural beauty. The area has a few historic sites and various other attractions of interest to travelers. Travelers who like the open air will typically enjoy visiting the area's outdoor parks and botanical garden. Those wanting to find out more about area sightseeing opportunities can do so by visiting reading on Attractions page in this book.

Snorkeling

If spending some time snorkeling sounds like fun you'll be pleased to know you'll have plenty of chances to do so within easy reach of Paradise Island. To read our detailed guide to local snorkeling opportunities, read on Snorkeling page in this book.

Spas

Indulging in a trip to the spa might be one of the highlights of your vacation. It shouldn't be hard to find a spa you like, considering that there are 5 spas that operate in this area. Read on Spas page in this book which is all about spas in the area if you want to find out additional specifics.

Tennis

If you enjoy playing tennis your best bet is to stay at a hotel with a tennis court. Fortunately, there are 6 properties in the area that offer tennis.

The following information may help with you make a decision. Included is the number of tennis courts on-site, whether lights are available for evening play, and some other details. Click on each name to read more details concerning the property.

ACCOMMODATIONS WITH TENNIS ON PARADISE ISLAND				
Property	Location	Tennis Courts	Lit Courts	Tennis Pro
Atlantis Royal Towers	Central Paradise Island	2		
Atlantis Coral Towers	Central Paradise Island	6		
One & Only Ocean Club	Central Paradise Island	6		
Atlantis The Cove	Central Paradise Island	6		
Atlantis Beach Tower	Central Paradise Island	6		

Atlantis The Reef	Central Paradise Island	6		

For instance, Atlantis Royal Towers offers all-inclusive pricing, to help simplify your vacation.

Other Activities

Details concerning some other activities are summarized directly below.

OTHER ACTIVITIES ON AND AROUND PARADISE ISLAND			
Name	Type	Phone	Location
Aquadventure	Amusement/Theme Park	(242) 363-3000	Central Paradise Island
Dolphin Encounter	Dolphin Encounter Service	(242) 363-1003	3.7 mi. East-Northeast of Central Potters Cay
Mario's Bowling & Family	Bowling Center	326-8010	2.8 mi. West-Northwest of Central Nassau

Diving

Scuba Diving Near Paradise Island

With easy access to the Great Bahama Bank, diving from this destination is an adventure. Sites range from shallow reefs, a 200-foot wide natural opening called the Lost Blue Hole, and several shipwrecks. Many hotels on the island offer introductory diving, and there are a few operators available take those with a bit of training out to see what wonders are hidden beneath the surface of the sea.

You'll find dive services dive operators and at least 6 different dive sites to choose from.

Dive Operators

If you want to go diving, you should consider Custom Aquatics. Offering the most personalized, VIP experience on the island, Custom Aquatics aims to make your scuba diving adventure like nothing you've every experienced before. From the time you're picked up by your private driver to the time you return, every moment is carefully crafted to make sure you have the very best time possible. They are found in Cable Beach, West of Paradise Island.

Another good option is Sandals Royal Bahamian Divers. If you've never dived before, you can sign up for certification course for one day of your stay at Sandals, then get out on the water for a 40 foot open water tank dive the next day. There are also specialized dives for those who have been previously certified. They can be reached at (242) 327-6400.

The following chart has some key facts regarding the area's dive services.

DIVE OPERATORS NEAR PARADISE ISLAND		
Name	Phone	Location
Custom Aquatics	(242) 362-1492	3.6 mi. Northwest of Central Nassau
Sandals Royal Bahamian Divers	(242) 327-6400	0.0 mi. South-Southeast of Central Cable Beach

Dive Sites

The following chart enables you to learn some key facts concerning some of the area's major dive sites.

DIVE SITES NEAR PARADISE ISLAND				
Name	Quality	Max Depth	Latitude	Longitude
Athol Island Dive	--	--	25.0780778297	-77.2869515419
Atlantis Beach Diving	--	--	25.0899203866	-77.3220589757
Cabbage Beach Dive	--	--	25.0879989337	-77.3085486889
Montagu Bay Diving	--	--	25.0744434533	-77.3043966293
Paradise Rocks	--	--	25.0918272348	-77.3189556599

The Lighthouse	Good	59.1	25.0875	-77.3500666667

To learn more about diving, including suggestions and helpful tips for both "old pros" and beginners, check out this detailed about diving in the Caribbean online.

Nightlife

Nightlife on Paradise Island

On the weekends especially, Paradise Island's nightlife scene is hopping and the best thing about it is the options are so varied that no matter your party style, there is something for you here.

A casino, several dance clubs, and endless bars mean you can eat, drink, gamble, dance, and simply relax and have fun. Some bars are loud and boisterous, others are elegant, and still others are the epitome of an island bar with open air seating, a view of the beach, and a laid back style. There is even a bar on the Atlantis Resort property that was made specifically for teens vacationing on the island.

Meanwhile, live music is always going on somewhere, with both local and international acts up for the challenge of entertaining discerning guests from around the world

You'll find a fair number of a fair number of and a gambling site near Paradise Island.

If you want to go out for the evening, you should consider Atlantis Casino. It is situated in central Paradise Island. Stop by and try to win big at the Atlantis Casino. With nearly 1000 games going on at once, you can be sure there will be something for you, be it slots, or table games.

A second place worth considering is Aura. The lounge has plenty of dancing and music, though many come here simply for a drink. You can also purchase VIP Service so you'll be treated extra well. You can call them at (242) 363-3000.

A third place worth considering is Edgewater Bar. Get in the spirits with the specialty tropical drinks here, or just have a beer or two. Either way, this fully stocked bar will be able to make you something refreshing and tasty. They're located in Cable Beach, West of Paradise Island.

The chart right below lists some details concerning 6 venues for after-hours relaxation.

GAMBLING AND NIGHTLIFE ON AND AROUND PARADISE ISLAND			
Name	Type	Phone	Location

Atlantis Casino	Casino	(242) 363-3000		Central Paradise Island
Aura	Bar	(242) 363-3000		Central Paradise Island
Dune Bar	Bar	--		Central Paradise Island
Edgewater Bar	Bar	(242) 327-6000		0.7 mi. East of Central Cable Beach
The Daiquiri Shack	Bar	--		0.6 mi. East-Southeast of Central Cable Beach
The Telegraph Bar	Bar	(242) 327-6000		0.7 mi. East-Southeast of Central Cable Beach

Shopping on Paradise Island

Some of the trendiest, most luxurious, and high-end shopping in the Bahamas can be done on Paradise Island. Between the Shops at Atlantis and the Marina Village, you'll be able to stock up on high fashion, jewelry, house wares, fragrances, and more, and thanks to this being a duty free port, you can do it all at low prices.

For a more down-to-earth shopping experience, check out the Craft Center which is located right near the bridge from New Providence to

Paradise Island. You'll find a lot of great souvenirs here that commemorate your time in the Bahamas.

And, if you can't get enough of, take the bridge over the Nassau and continue your shopping adventures there. In addition to malls and boutiques they have the largest Straw Market in the Caribbean where you can stock up on local crafts and souvenirs.

Specialty Shops

One of the interesting speciality shops in the area is Havana Humidor. This store is located within central Paradise Island. As the name may suggests, Havana Humidor carries Cuban Cigars, in addition to local and international ones. If you do decide to buy a Cuba Cigar, remember that no Cuban products are allowed into the United States, and could be confiscated. If you want to call ahead of time, do so at (242) 363-5809.

Another good option is Quantum Marina Village, which is found within a mile to the east-southeast of Havana Humidor. Shop your heart's content at this duty free retailer of fine jewelry and genuine leather products. You can contact them at (242) 363-1247.

View the following table for more information about specialty shops serving Paradise Island.

SPECIALTY SHOPS ON PARADISE ISLAND			
Name	Type	Phone	Location
Colombian Emeralds Paradise Island	Jewelry Store	(242) 363-0347	Central Paradise Island
Doongalik	Art Gallery	(242) 394-1886	Central Paradise Island
Havana Humidor	Tobacconist and Cigar Shop	(242) 363-5809	Central Paradise Island
Paradise Blue Surf Shop	Surfing Gear Store	(242) 363-7263	Central Paradise Island
Park Lane Jewelers	Jewelry Store	(242) 363-1234	Central Paradise Island
Quantum Marina Village	Jewelry Store	(242) 363-1247	Central Paradise Island
Solomon's Mines Coral Towers	Jewelry Store	(242) 363-3616	Central Paradise Island
Solomon's Mines Royal Towers	Jewelry Store	(242) 363-5256	Central Paradise Island

Clothing and Apparel

Hoping to find some new clothing during your vacation? You might enjoy a visit to Piraña Joe -- which is located within central Paradise

Island. There's something wild about each piece of clothing and accessory you purchase from Pirana Joe -- quite like the company's owners who thrive on adventure and the outdoors. Stop in and take a shop on the wild side. If you want to call before you go, you can do so at (242) 326-8856.

A second good option is Gucci Store Atlantis -- which is located within a mile to the west of Piraña Joe. Imported from Italy, these fashion designer bags are a coveted product among women around the world, and this store at Atlantis sells them direct. Visitors can find them on Crystal Court.

A third option for clothing is Escape at the Cove. Shop around at Escape At The Cove, and take a look at the skillfully made clothing that is sure to attract attention. If you want to know more, call them at (242) 363-3000.

A variety of apparel shops located on Paradise Island are displayed in the following table.

CLOTHING AND APPAREL ON PARADISE ISLAND

Name	Type	Phone	Location
A La Plage	Boutique	(242) 363-7263	Central Paradise Island

Calypso Carousel	Boutique	(242) 263-0380	Central Island	Paradise
Escape at the Cove	Boutique	(242) 363-3000	Central Island	Paradise
Gucci Store Atlantis	Clothing Accessory and Handbag Store	(242) 363-5823	Central Island	Paradise
Piraña Joe	T-Shirt Shop	(242) 326-8856	Central Island	Paradise
Sunglass Shack	Sunglasses Shop	--	Central Island	Paradise

Food and Grocery

Looking for some food? Tortuga Rum Cakes is situated in central Paradise Island. In addition to rum cakes, this location sells chocolates, coffees, and other gifts. You can contact them at (242) 326-1680.

A second place to consider is Original Swiss Sweet Shop, which is located 5.5 mi. (8.9 km) from Tortuga Rum Cakes. Trained in Switzerland and other countries in Europe, owner and executive pastry chef Armin Wernli has just the right experience needed to create Swiss-style breads, pastries, cakes, and other desserts. You can contact them at (242) 327-5836.

View this table to learn more.

FOOD AND GROCERY STORES ON PARADISE ISLAND			
Name	Type	Phone	Location
City Market	Fruit and Vegetable Market	--	0.2 mi. South West of Central Cable Beach
Green Convenience Store	Convenience Store	--	3.7 mi. East-Northeast of Central Nassau
Liquid Courage	Beer, Wine, and Liquor Store	(242) 327-2202	0.7 mi. West of Central Cable Beach
Original Swiss Sweet Shop	Bakery	(242) 327-5836	0.2 mi. East-Southeast of Central Cable Beach
Super Value	Grocery Store	--	0.8 mi. West of Central Cable Beach
Tortuga Rum Cakes	Bakery	(242) 326-1680	Central Paradise Island

Other Retail
Another 7 shops are listed here:

OTHER TYPES OF SHOPPING ON PARADISE ISLAND			
Name	Type	Phone	Location
Bahama Craft Center	Shopping Center	--	0.3 mi. Northeast of Central

			Potters Cay
Cable Beach Shopping Center	Shopping Center	--	0.1 mi. South-Southwest of Central Cable Beach
Le Perfumerie	Cosmetics and Perfume Store	--	Central Paradise Island
Marina Village	Shopping Center	--	Central Paradise Island
Paradise Blue Surf Shop	Surfing Gear Store	(242) 363-7263	Central Paradise Island
Paradise Shopping Plaza	Shopping Center	--	Central Paradise Island
Shoppes of Cable Beach	Shopping Center	--	0.7 mi. West of Central Cable Beach

Snorkeling Around Paradise Island

A visit to Paradise Island is a unique "island paradise" experience, even in the realm of the Bahamas. The whole island is so catered to tourism that your every moment can be booked ahead of time, whether you're hitting the water parks, sunning on the beach, or testing your luck in the casino. It can be easy to overlook some of the best things about Paradise Island, but one activity you'll want to take special care to plan is snorkeling.

The location of Paradise Island puts it at the Tongue of the Ocean and the shallows of the Great Bahama Bank. This makes the waters different than anywhere else around the world, and means that snorkeling will be an experience you cannot compare. In these waters you'll experience gorgeous coral reefs overflowing with equally as gorgeous fish, blue holes, shipwrecks, caverns, caves and more.

If you're new to snorkeling, see if you can gain access to the Atlantis Lagoons, where the waters are calm and shallow and great for even children. Whether new or well-versed on the ins and outs of snorkeling, you can never go wrong hiring one of the local guides to show you the best sites. And, if you have a friend planning a day of scuba diving, ask about tagging along to do some snorkeling. Most diver operations offer this service at a minimal fee.

Snorkeling Sites

If you'd like to see what's below the surface you should consider a visit to Atlantis Lagoons. The lagoons at this popular resort are the man-made site with purposely sunken artifacts and colorful fish brought in to create a snorkeling opportunity for guests. It is ideal for those new to the sport as well as young children, but in truth there is not much for an experienced snorkeler to see. This snorkeling site is located in the central part of Paradise Island.

Gambier Deep Reef is another option. Although this reef system goes as deep as 80 feet below the surface, the upper coral formations are a great spot for snorkelers to see a healthy amount of marine life.

A third location to consider is Fish Hotel. A reef system that goes as deep as 45 feet down, this collection of coral serves as a great home to the various fish that come and go here including grunts, snappers, goatfish, angels, and more. Lobsters can also be spotted on occasion.

Take a moment to look through the table below for a summary list of 3 of the best places to go snorkeling in this area.

SNORKELING SITES NEAR PARADISE ISLAND	
Site	Location
Atlantis Lagoons	Central Paradise Island
Fish Hotel	6.9 mi. Northeast of Central Nassau
Gambier Deep Reef	6.9 mi. Northwest of Central Nassau

Snorkeling Boat Trips

For some people, the best snorkeling is experienced away from the shore.

If you're ready to combine some snorkeling with a boating adventure, you can check with Flying Cloud. For something different, why not have dinner on board a sail boat? Or perhaps you would rather take a lunch picnic at a deserted beach?

A few details about the opportunity to take a boat ride that includes snorkeling are provided in the following chart.

DAY SAILS AND BOAT TRIPS ON PARADISE ISLAND				
Name	Type	Phone	Location	Island
Flying Cloud	Boating and Day-Sailing Provider	(242) 394-5067	1.3 mi. East of Central downtown Nassau	New Providence

The magic of Paradise Island extends off the coast, where there is a whole world to be seen just below the surface. Don't allow yourself to miss out on this great adventure by forgetting to plan an afternoon spent snorkeling.

Spas in Paradise Island

On Paradise Island you'll find the largest spa in the islands is located at the Atlantis Resort, but there are also a few other smaller facilities if you dream of a more personalized experience. The spas here tend to favor European treatment methods, and have packages for both couples and singletons alike.

Spa-goers will find plenty of options, given the fact that there are 5 spas that operate in this area.

If you're ready to unwind, you might want to contact One&Only Ocean Club Spa. One of the finest spas in the region, One&Only; is also an award winning facility where you can go for relaxation, beautification, and realistic healing. They are located in central Paradise Island.

A second option is Hair International Salon & Spa. With a commitment to offer the highest quality of service for guests staying at the Melia Nassau Beach Resort and anyone who comes in off the street, Hair International is a full service salon and spa, bringing beauty and peace to the mind, body, spirit, and without a doubt, the hair. They can be reached at (242) 327-3558.

Still another option is Mandara Spa At Atlantis. With traditional European spa therapies blended with Asia's ancient techniques, Mandara Spa, a 30,000 square feet facility, is most likely the largest spa in all of the Bahamas. They take the best of each region and bring them together to create an impressive line up of treatments. They're located within central Paradise Island.

Glance through the following table for a few key facts concerning local establishments.

SPAS ON AND AROUND PARADISE ISLAND		
Name	Phone	Location
ESPA	(242) 788-1234	1.0 mi. Southeast of Central Cable Beach
Hair International Salon & Spa	(242) 327-3558	0.7 mi. East-Southeast of Central Cable Beach
Mandara Spa At Atlantis	(242) 363-3000	Central Paradise Island
Marley Spa	(242) 702-2800	0.3 mi. East of Central Cable Beach
One & Only Ocean Club Spa	(242) 363-2000	Central Paradise Island

Accommodation

Paradise Island Accommodation Options

When people think of Paradise Island, they generally think of large properties that have the "go big" attitude, but that isn't all you'll find here. Also on the island are smaller, standard hotels and even a few villa complexes set along the shore.

Hotels

There are multiple property types to choose from on the island, including a few hotels and a variety of resorts. Those looking to enjoy a spirited bar scene will find precisely that at a handful hotels around Paradise Island. Read further information regarding each property by clicking the links.

One of the best spots on Paradise Island for convenient dining is Comfort Suites Paradise Island. Comfort Suites Paradise Island is an affordable getaway for families traveling to the Bahamas. Not only is the hotel within a reasonable distance to many of Nassau's most popular attractions, but kids stay, eat, and play free at the hotel.

A place located on the coast that merits your consideration is One & Only Ocean Club. Originally a private estate that was transformed into a hotel in 1962, One&Only; Ocean Club has evolved into a luxurious resort with two sprawling wings and separate villas and cottages. Guests will find themselves sleeping amidst fragrant tropical gardens, while the sandy white beach is just steps away. If you are looking to call before booking a room, do so at (242) 363-2501.

If you are wanting to find a property with a lively late-night scene, Club Land'or Resort is one location you may want to think about. Named for the Land of Gold on Paradise Island, Club Land'or is a unique clubhouse-style resort comprised completely of villas. Guests of the villas will have plenty of activities to enjoy like the Bahamian Dance and BBQ, or explore the sights of downtown Nassau, just minutes away. To talk to them, call (242) 363-2400.

Condos and Villa Complexes

There are non-hotel booking options on and near Paradise Island, which include a condominium building and some villa complexes. Avid beach-goers can usually expect to enjoy convenient access to the beach, as a lot of the properties are right on the water.

For vacationers wanting to stay somewhere with a good bar and club scene, Atlantis Harborside Resort is one destination you might want to consider. Enjoy the best of both worlds at the cheerfully colorful Harborside Resort at Atlantis. Lavish seaside villas afford guests privacy, while just steps away is the famed Atlantis Resort. You can contact them at (242) 363-6800.

A property positioned on the water's edge that is worth considering is Sunrise Beach Club & Villas. Sunrise Beach Villas is a resort located on Paradise Island. This property is relaxing enough for a family vacation and romantic enough for weddings and honeymoons. If you're looking for something specific, try calling them at (800) 451-6078.

Another property worth considering is Westwind II by Evrentals. Located on the edge of Cable Beach on Nassau Island in the Bahamas, the Westwind II Club is a time-share resort set in the midst of a tropical paradise. Rooms are available with optional views and amenities. If you are looking to call ahead of time, you can do so at (242) 327-7211.

Individual Villas

Some would rather have the privacy offered by one of the privately rented villas. For more details about the individual villa rentals on and around Paradise Island, search online Bahamas"Villa Rentals".

All-Inclusive Accommodations

Some travelers love the advantages of an all-inclusive price. There are many reasons why these plans are so popular. For example, they avoid the need to prepare a detailed budget.

Tennis enthusiasts and their families often like the idea of staying at Atlantis Royal Towers, as they have some nice tennis facilities. All of the guest rooms at Atlantis Royal Towers are outfitted in Bahamian decor. Each room comes with unique touches such as French balconies and terraces, and full service bars. Call them at (242) 363-3000.

One place on the waterfront that is worth considering is Riu Palace Paradise Island. The Riu Palace Paradise Island is an all-inclusive resort situated on a three-mile stretch of Atlantic Ocean beachfront. Guests can lounge by the pool, sunbathe on the sun terrace, work out in the state-of-the-art gym, and connect to the Internet in the Wireless LAN zone. You will be able to find them at 6307 Casino Drive.

All Inclusive

All Inclusive Resorts on Paradise Island

Paradise Island is home to one of the most popular all-inclusive resorts in all of the Bahamas: Atlantis Paradise Island. What many people don't know is that it is not the only all-inclusive in the area. Another resort on the island caters to adults and is known for its exclusivity, and if you cross the bridge you'll find a much larger collection on New Providence.

Some people like the reassurance of paying for everything on a single bill. There are multiple explanations why this pricing method is popular. As an example, they allow you to know in advance what your vacation will cost. Navigate to the different ones to get more information on activities, amenities, food, and more.

If you're interested in an active late-night scene, Atlantis Harborside Resort is one spot you might want to think about. One, two, and three bedroom villas with full kitchens and master suite with whirlpool tub are available for guests to choose from at Harborside Resort at Atlantis. All rooms have an open, airy design which allows guests to enjoy the warm breezes that float from the harbor. If you want to call before booking a room, do so at (242) 363-6800.

One destination along the ocean that you could consider is Atlantis Coral Towers. One of the most famous resorts in the world, Atlantis will take guests out of the real world and transport them to a water-themed fantasy. The luxurious amenities make guests feel like royalty, and the endless activities are sure to entertain. For customers who want to call before making reservations, do so at (954) 809-2100.

Travelers who are in search of convenient on-location dining might want to think about Atlantis The Cove. Inspired by the beauty of its surroundings between two of the most spectacular beaches in the Bahamas, The Cove Atlantis is beautiful and sophisticated. Known as one of the top resorts in the Caribbean, Conde Nast Traveler confirmed this in 2013 with a readers choice vote that placed it at number eight in its category that matched it up against all of the hotels on Bermuda, Turks and Caicos, and the Bahamas. You can call them at (877) 268-3847.

Many all-inclusive choices available on the island are provided in the table below.

ALL-INCLUSIVE ACCOMMODATIONS ON PARADISE ISLAND				
Name	Type	Phone Number	Star Rating	Location
Atlantis Beach Tower	Resort	(242) 363-3000		Central Paradise Island
Atlantis Coral Towers	Hotel	(954) 809-2100		Central Paradise Island
Atlantis Harborside Resort	Villa complex	(242) 363-6800		Central Paradise Island
Atlantis Royal Towers	Resort	(242) 363-3000		Central Paradise Island
Atlantis The Cove	Resort	(877) 268-3847		Central Paradise Island
Atlantis The Reef	Resort	(242) 363-3000		Central Paradise Island
Riu Palace Paradise Island	Hotel	(242) 363-3500		Central Paradise Island
Sivananda Ashram Yoga Retreat	Resort	(242) 363-2902		0.8 mi. Northeast of Central downtown Nassau

The fine print is that many of them offer different levels of quality and amenities under the title of all-inclusive. It's best to do a little research to see what is included in each location's fee.

Hotels

Hotels on Paradise Island
Paradise Island is one of the most tourist friendly islands in the Bahamas. Hotel and resort properties here take care of everything from food to entertainment, and many properties have erected stages for shows and even built waterparks for guests to take advantage of.

Hotels On Paradise Island

There are multiple categories of hotels to choose between on the island, including a few hotels and plenty of resorts. Guests wanting to enjoy a lively late-night scene will encounter exactly that at a handful hotels around Paradise Island. Click on the links to read additional details.

One of the best spots on Paradise Island to enjoy on-site dining is Riu Palace Paradise Island. The Riu Palace Paradise Island is an all-inclusive resort situated on a three-mile stretch of Atlantic Ocean beachfront. Guests can lounge by the pool, sunbathe on the sun terrace, work out in the state-of-the-art gym, and connect to the Internet in the Wireless LAN zone. They're located at 6307 Casino Drive.

One destination on the coast with excellent views of the water is Atlantis Coral Towers. One of the most famous resorts in the world, Atlantis will take guests out of the real world and transport them to a water-themed fantasy. The luxurious amenities make guests feel like royalty, and the endless activities are sure to entertain. If you have questions and want to call in advance, you can do so at (954) 809-2100.

Those who appreciate convenient on-site dining might want to consider One & Only Ocean Club. Originally a private estate that was transformed into a hotel in 1962, One&Only; Ocean Club has evolved into a luxurious resort with two sprawling wings and separate villas and cottages. Guests will find themselves sleeping amidst fragrant tropical gardens, while the sandy white beach is just steps away. To contact them, call (242) 363-2501.

The table directly below lists a few details concerning hotel possibilities.

HOTELS ON PARADISE ISLAND				
Name	Type	Phone	Star	Location

		Number	Rating	
Atlantis Beach Tower	Resort	(242) 363-3000		Central Paradise Island
Atlantis Coral Towers	Hotel	(954) 809-2100		Central Paradise Island
Atlantis Royal Towers	Resort	(242) 363-3000		Central Paradise Island
Atlantis The Cove	Resort	(877) 268-3847		Central Paradise Island
Atlantis The Reef	Resort	(242) 363-3000		Central Paradise Island
Best Western Bay View Suites	Hotel	(242) 363-2555		1.7 mi. East of Central downtown Nassau
Club Land'or Resort	Hotel	(242) 363-2400		3.8 mi. Northeast of Central Nassau
Comfort Suites Paradise Island	Resort	--		Central Paradise Island
One & Only Ocean Club	Resort	(242) 363-2501		Central Paradise Island
Paradise Harbour Club & Marina	Resort	(242) 363-2992		3.9 mi. Northeast of Central Nassau
Paradise Island Beach Club	Hotel	(242) 363-0101		2.2 mi. East of Central downtown Nassau

Riu Palace Paradise Island	Hotel	(242) 363-3500		Central Paradise Island
Sivananda Ashram Yoga Retreat	Resort	(242) 363-2902		0.8 mi. Northeast of Central downtown Nassau

Luckily, you'll be able to find some other types of properties you can find. For more information concerning other kinds of accommodations for Paradise Island, go to "Accommodation page in this book.

Transportation to Paradise Island

Paradise Island Transportation Options

There are more transportation options on Paradise Island than you might imagine given its size

Connected to New Providence by two 600-foot bridges, many tourists agree that Paradise Island wholly lives up to its name. Home to the mega-resort Atlantis Paradise Island, everything one could ask for in a tropical getaway is available on this tiny island that is only five miles long and one mile wide. Getting to the island required either a trip over the bridge or a ferry ride, then once you are there you can walk everywhere, rely on public transportation, or rent a car to get around.

Getting There

Guests staying at Atlantis Paradise Island often fly into New Providence thanks to promotional pricing packages that include air travel. Others will have to choose between flying and sailing, and cruising to Nassau then crossing the bridge to Paradise Island is a possibility as well.

Getting Around

While renting a vehicle may seem like the most natural solution for your transportation needs on Paradise Island, it simply is not a necessity. Consider taxi, bus, and ferry services are valid options as well.

Air Travel

The airport nearest Paradise Island is the Lynden Pindling International Airport just eight miles outside of Nassau on New Providence Island. This airport is the only international airport in the island chain and is quite busy welcoming flights for people staying on New Providence Island and heading elsewhere in the island chain. Tourists staying on New Providence Island will only have to travel a half an hour after arriving at the airport, making this a great option for the first leg of your trip.

Commercial airlines from around the world are known to frequent this airport on a daily basis, so no matter where you're traveling from, you won't find it a difficult task to book a flight to th[...]

paradise.Click here for more information and a full list of airl[...]

Sailing

Flying into the airport on New Providence and taking a taxi to Paradise Island can be expensive. While sailing your own boat or setting up a charter might not always be cheaper, you will have a much more rich experience.

Those who do decide to sail to the Bahamas will find some docks at Paradise Island, though some other nearby options on Potters Cay will probably work better. Additionally, before leaving, it will be a good idea to head over to Nassau and restock your supplies, as Nassau is regarded as the best place in the Bahamas to do this.

Finally, sailing is not limited to people with their own boats. There are a number of excursion and charter companies in the area that tourist can use to experience the seas and maritime activiites Paradise Island and the Bahamas have to offer.

Cruising

The Prince George Wharf, which is located in the middle of Downtown Nassau is a popular stop for Caribbean cruisers, and many will head over to Paradise Island as part of an excursion hosted by the cruise, or just on their own to explore. The great number of sea life

irk and beaches make Paradise Island
ke to make sure visiting his island is on
book your cruise which are known for
nd.

Rental Cars

Most agree than renting a car on Paradise Island is completely unnecessary given the small size of the island and the ease of public transportation, however, that doesn't mean you can't rent a car if it something you need or want to do. Rentals can be obtained directly from the airport, or you can take a taxi or the ferry over to Paradise Island and rent a vehicle when you arrive at your hotel. Driving on the island shouldn't cause you any strife, but what you will have to get used to driving on the left side of the road if you're from the United States. Learn more about renting a car and driving on Paradise Island, read on Rental Cars page in this book.

Taxis

Taxis are probably the most popular way for tourists staying on Paradise Island to get around the small stretch of land outside of walking. You'll find drivers waiting outside of resorts, by the beach, and nearby all of the most popular attractions. One of the most important things you need to know about taking a taxi here is that if you need to go over the bridge, you will be responsible for the $1(USD) bridge toll. Always make sure to agree upon your fare before your start driving. Some drivers charge a set rate while others have meters, so it is best to hammer out all of the details in advance. Read on Taxis page in this book.

Buses

When you want to take a break from the laid back lifestyle you'll encounter on Paradise Island, you can head across the bridge to the main island of New Providence Island and explore the island by bus. Between the hours of 6:30 a.m. and 7:00 a.m. each day, the public bus runs, offering rides for just $1.50(USD) per person each way. The most popular route is the number 10 bus, which runs by Fort Charlotte, Ardastra Gardens, and the Cable Beach resorts. Other routes make stops by the popular beaches, restaurants, and shopping centers among other things. Take note, most buses will not cross the bus over to Paradise Island. They will however drop you off at the base of the bridge and allow you to walk across.

Ferries

The ferry you'll be most concerned with for your stay is the ferry to and from Paradise Island. This ferry travels from the center of Nassau to Paradise Island non-stop. There is no set schedule, rather the ferry just continues to move back and forth between the two stops on a trip that lasts 20 minutes. Passengers pay $3(USD) each way. If you have plans to visit other islands in the chain, read on Ferry to Nassau page in this book to learn more about ferry services around the Bahamas.

When you plan a trip to a place called Paradise Island, it's obvious what type of vacation you're after. Your serene, tropical getaway will be made even better if you've ironed out all of the details before you arrive. This includes making simple plans such as how you'll get to and around the small island. Take the time to go through your options now and you'll thank yourself later

Air Travel to Paradise Island

Paradise Island, New Providence's premier resort town, is serviced by the Lynden Pindling International Airport

Paradise Island is almost primarily used by tourists as a grand resort town for those looking for adventure, fun, and a true tropical getaway. The island itself is connected to New Providence by bridge, and most people will begin their vacation by first flying into the local airport before making the 30 minute drive to their accommodations.

At less than an hour away by plane from the state of Florida, the Bahamas is easily accessible by people from the United States. It is probably for this reason that over 80 percent of people who pass through the Lynden Pindling International Airport each year do so from the United States. Still, international flights from North America, South America, Europe, and Asia touchdown at LPIO every day, and tourists from around the world will not have trouble booking a flight with the major commercial airlines that are known to fly to the Bahamas.

Tourists should always be prepared with their passport as well as a secondary form of identification when traveling to the Bahamas, because even though several countries such as Canada, the United Kingdom, and the United States are exempt from presenting their passports for a short stay on the islands, citizens will still need to present their passports to re-enter their home country.

Island Hopping

If you've got some extra time on your hands, chances are you're planning to take a day or two to do some island-hopping. If this is the case, you have two options with regards to how you'll fly. The first is to travel aboard BahamasAir, the most popular domestic airline. They offer flights every day to 14 different islands, and even a few to spots in the United States. With BahamasAir, your flight will be similar to ones booked about commercial airlines, just on a smaller scale, and seats are booked individually.

Your other option is to hire a private charter, also known as a Fixed-Base Operator (FBO). This is a great option if you're traveling with a larger party because you pay for the plane as a whole, rather than per seat. It is also ideal if you want to fly to an island not listed as a destination with BahamasAir.

Private Plane

Private planes are more than welcome to make the journey from Miami to FPIA, so long as they make sure to get all of the proper paperwork in order and follow the appropriate steps. They are as follows:

➢ Prepare and file your International Flight Plan.

➢ Use Miami radio frequencies 122.2, 122.4, or 126.7 to activate your flight plan.

➢ Switch over to Nassau radio frequencies 124.2 or 128.0 when you approach to close out your flight plan.

When you arrive in the Bahamas, you will need to present three copies of the C71 Bahamas Customs form, proof of citizenship, and a

Bahamas Immigration Card. Meanwhile, your return to the United States will have some subtle differences. Your to do list will be as follows:

➤ Complete a Gen Dec.

➤ Turn in a copy of your Immigration Card.

➤ File your International Flight Plan at 800-WXBRIEF.

➤ Use the Nassau radio frequencies noted above to activate your flight.

➤ Listen to WOR 116.7 during your flight.

➤ Switch to FDD 126.7 Miami Radio as you approach the city to obtain your discrete transporder code.

➤ Close at your flight with 126.7 Miami Radio.

A quick call to the Avian Specialist Department at the Bahamas Ministry of Tourism will clear up any questions you have about the process. The can be contacted at 800-32-SPORT.

Getting to Paradise Island from the Airport

Several options exist for tourists who land in New Providence Island and need to get over the bridge to Paradise Island. The first is to rent a carand to drive yourself. If you'll spend your entire trip on Paradise Island, this is not recommended because the area is so tourist-friendly that there are plenty of ways to get around the island without having to driver yourself. Most people choose to hire a taxi. As previously noted, the trip takes 30 minutes and will cost about $32(USD) plus a $1(USD) bridge toll and the cost of a tip. Your final option is to take a $6(USD) ferry from Nassau to Paradise Island. These ferries depart from Prince George Wharf and take 10 minutes to reach Paradise Island. The last option is fun, but will still require a 20 minute taxi ride from the airport.

Getting to Paradise Island by air is one of the easiest options out there, though you'll have to travel about a half an hour after you arrive on New Providence to get there. Even so, it is the most popular transportation choice, and one you should wholeheartedly consider.

For those who live in the United States this list can aid the planning process. Not all of the flights you will be shown on the web make a lot of sense so it's useful to see a summary of which airlines provide direct service to this airport.

LYNDEN PINDLING INTERNATIONAL AIRPORT U.S. FLIGHTS		
To/From	Airport Code	Airlines
Baltimore, MD, USA	BWI	AirTran, US Airways
Detroit, MI, USA	DTW	KLM, US Airways

Fort Lauderdale, FL, USA	FLL	Bahamasair, Jet Blue, SkyBahamas
Manchester, NH, USA	MHT	US Airways
Miami, FL, USA	MIA	American Eagle, Bahamasair
New Orleans, LA, USA	MSY	US Airways
Orlando, FL, USA	MCO	Bahamasair, Jet Blue
St. Louis, MO, USA	STL	US Airways
West Palm Beach, FL, USA	PBI	Bahamasair
Windsor Locks, CT, USA	BDL	US Airways

This chart indicates airline companies that have direct service from Canadian cities.

LYNDEN PINDLING INTERNATIONAL AIRPORT CANADIAN FLIGHTS		
To/From	Airport Code	Airlines
Montreal, Canada	YUL	Air Canada

Flying to Paradise Island from the Caribbean

Check the chart below for airline service from airports in the Caribbean region. If you can't get a flight directly from your local airport, taking a connecting flight from another airport might be your best option.

LYNDEN PINDLING INTERNATIONAL AIRPORT CARIBBEAN FLIGHTS		
To/From	Airport Code	Airlines
Abaco, Bahamas	MHH	Abaco Air, Bahamasair, SkyBahamas, Western Air
Abaco, Bahamas	TCB	Bahamasair
Acklins, Bahamas	AXP	Bahamasair
Acklins, Bahamas	CRI	Bahamasair
Andros, Bahamas	COX	Performance Air, Western Air
Andros, Bahamas	MAY	Flamingo Air, Performance Air
Andros, Bahamas	SAQ	Western Air
Cat Island, Bahamas	ATC	SkyBahamas
Cat Island, Bahamas	CAT	SkyBahamas
Eleuthera, Bahamas	ELH	Bahamasair, SkyBahamas
Eleuthera, Bahamas	GHB	Bahamasair
Freeport, Grand Bahama Island	FPO	Bahamasair, SkyBahamas, Western Air
Georgetown, Grand Cayman	GCM	British Airways
Great Exuma, Bahamas	GGT	Bahamasair, SkyBahamas

Havana, Cuba	HAV	Bahamasair
Inagua, Bahamas	IGA	Bahamasair
Kingston, Jamaica	KTP	Caribbean Airlines
Long Island, Bahamas	LGI	Bahamasair, SkyBahamas
Long Island, Bahamas	SML	Bahamasair, SkyBahamas
Mayaguana, Bahamas	MYG	Bahamasair
Normans Cay, Bahamas	NMC	Performance Air
Providenciales, Turks and Caicos Islands	PLS	Bahamasair, British Airways, Intercaribbean Airways
Rock Sound, Eleuthera	RSD	Bahamasair
San Salvador, Bahamas	ZSA	Bahamasair, SkyBahamas
Staniel Cay, Bahamas	TYM	Flamingo Air, Performance Air
the Bahamas	MYE3	Flamingo Air
the Bahamas	MYEB	Flamingo Air
the Berry Islands, Bahamas	GHC	SkyBahamas
the Bimini Islands, Bahamas	BIM	SkyBahamas, Western Air

Getting to Paradise Island by air is one of the easiest options out there, though you'll have to travel about a half an hour after you arrive on New Providence to get there. Even so, it is the most popular transportation choice, and one you should wholeheartedly consider.

Paradise Island Ferries

Skip driving across the bridge and take the Paradise Island Ferry instead

Ferries are one of the most important forms of transportation in the Bahamas, and Paradise Island is a great example of this. If you'll be staying on this island, you'll want to be aware of ferry services as one transportation option, plus, you'll want to know about some of the other ferry services that travel around the Bahamas as well.

Paradise Island Ferry

The most important ferry for guests who plan to stay on Paradise Island to be aware of is the Paradise Island Ferry. The island is set just off the northeast coast of New Providence, connected only by a toll bridge. Crossing the bridge is one way to get to Paradise Island, but many people choose to instead travel to the island aboard a ferry that runs all day, every day. It costs $3(USD) and runs from the middle of Nassau straight to Paradise Island. It takes about 20 minutes to sail between the two locations, and ferry service moves continually throughout the day meaning you'll never have to wait longer than 40 minutes for the next ferry.

Mail Boats

Originating from Potter's Cay, which is easily accessible just after the bridge between Paradise Island and the main land of New Providence, is the government run Mail Boat service, which offers freight, mail, and passenger transport between quite a collection of islands in the Bahamas.

Mail Boats are the least expensive ferry service between the islands, but the trade off is that they move very slowly. Tourists report the most success when they plan to travel between islands that are very near one another.

Fast Ferries

Servicing New Providence, the Abacos, Andros, Eleuthera, and the Exumas, Bahamas Fast Ferries is true to its name and offers quick transportation around the Bahamas. In fact, the service was created as a counter to the slower Mail Boat system. Each morning a fleet of ferries leaves New Providence and makes a stop at each island before returning back to Potter's Cay at 6:00 p.m.

Albury's Ferries

Albury's Ferries is a fleet of a dozen fiberglass boats called "donnies" that visit the collection of islands surrounding March Garbour each day. You can take this ferry to Marsh Harbour, Man-of-War, Hope Town, Guana, and Scotland on a daily basis.

Pinar del Rio

Sometimes referred to the Bahamas Express Ferry, Pinar del Rio offers transportation between Ft. Lauderdale, Florida and Freeport, Grand Bahama. The ferry runs daily, except for Wednesdays, leaving Florida at 10:00 a.m. and returning at 7:30 p.m. It takes two-and-a-half hours of sailing to get to either destination, but the $49.50(USD) price makes it a great option for a quick trip to the Bahamas. This is not the ideal way to get to Paradise Island, but it is a valid option for tourists visiting from Florida who don't mind getting a small domestic flight from Grand Bahama to Nassau after they arrive.

Paradise Island Ferry Terminal is the one dock for which we have information.

Ferries serve as a great way to connect between numerous islands in the Bahamas. Knowing what your options are helps you to decide which services you'll take advantage of and which you'll save for next time.

Renting a Car on Paradise Island

Drive yourself from place to place by renting a car for your stay on Paradise Island

Most people who plan their vacation on Paradise Island do so because of the all-inclusive nature of the island, and having a rental car at their disposal simply is not necessary. Tourists who need or still want to have a vehicle on hand, however, won't have much trouble getting behind the wheel.

Renting a Car

If you're going to rent a car for your stay on Paradise Island, it is recommended that you do so when you arrive at the airport. This will save you from having to take a taxi over the bridge and pay not only the cab fare but the bridge toll as well. There are numerous agencies set on airport property, so this shouldn't be a struggle. Still, if you'd rather have someone who knows the way get you to Paradise Island before you get behind the wheel, there are plenty of rental agencies across the bridge for you to choose from.

When you arrive, make sure to have a valid driver's license on hand. This will allow you to drive in the Bahamas for up to three months. If you plan to stay longer, apply for an International Driver's License well in advance of your trip and have it with you. Also, you'll need to be at least 21-years-old, and many agencies even require you to be 25. Call in advance to find out at what age the agency allows tourists to rent vehicles from them if you are worried.

Check out this table which lists the few area rental agencies.

VEHICLE RENTAL COMPANIES		
Name	Phone	Location
Avis Nassau Airport	(242) 377-7121	Lynden Pindling International Airport - 4.1 mi. (6.6 km) South West of Cable Beach
Budget Cars Nassau	(242) 377-9000	Lynden Pindling International Airport - 4.1 mi. (6.6 km) South West of Cable Beach
Dollar NAS Airport	(242) 377-8300	Lynden Pindling International Airport - 4.1 mi. (6.6 km) South West of Cable Beach

Driving around Paradise Island

Paradise Island is not overwhelmed with traffic like other areas of New Providence Island such as Nassau, so it is one of the better areas for tourists to get in the grove of driving on foreign soil. The most important thing to know about driving on the island is that traffic moves on the left side of the road, and roundabouts are frequently used to slow down traffic. Roads can be narrow, so be prepared to be packed in close to other cars as you drive.

Parking can be hard to find and you may end up having to park a reasonable distance away from your destination and walk. Gas is also a bit of a problem, with prices soaring well over $4(USD) a gallon regularly.

The Cost of Renting a Car

The cost of a rental on Paradise Island is anywhere from $80 to $120(USD) a day. The cost varies based upon where you rent from (local agencies tend to offer lower prices), when you rent (it is more expensive during the peak of tourist season), and the type of vehicle and amenities you request.

If you aren't keen on renting a full sized vehicle for your whole trip, consider renting a motor scooter for a day or two of sightseeing. These vehicles require less gas and are great for zipping around town as you explore, plus the cost is low. A full day rental, between the hours of 8:00 a.m. and 5:00 p.m. costs just $85(USD), and a half day is $65(USD).

Gas Stations

Since you could have problems spotting places to refuel, check out the chart just below to get a picture of where some of them are located.

GAS STATIONS

Name	Location
Sandyport Marina Gas St	Olde Town Sandyport
Shell	2.4 mi. (3.8 km) East of Cable Beach

Make sure to have a map or GPS system on hand to help you get around, or you may find that you are stopping to ask for directions frequently. Locals are friendly and helpful off the road, but once they get behind the wheel they can be a bit aggressive. Always wear your seat belt, buckle children into the appropriate child safety seats, and drive defensively

Boating and Sailing Near Paradise Island

Over 100,000 people sail to Nassau each year, and many people break off and sail over to Paradise Island
Linked to Nassau in nearly every way, even sailing is dependent on Nassau for most of the marina and entertainment options. Of course, there are a few luxury options available on Paradise Island, though they are all often overshadowed by other, cheaper options on New Providence.

Travel time between Miami, Florida and Paradise Island is somewhere between six and eight hours, and you'll need to fly your yellow quarantine flag as you near the island. You can contact port authority at VHF channel 16 to let them know you're on your way, and an official will meet with you to go over your proof of citizenship and help you to fill our your immigration forms when you arrive. Then, you will pay a fee of between $150 and $300(USD) depending upon the size of your vessel, for a cruising and fishing permit that covers up to four people.

If you're simply wanting to spend a few hours on the water, without the stress and cost associated with renting a boat you can take an excursion. Wanting to know more about day sailing options? See the table that follows for information on area day sailing companies.

BOAT EXCURSIONS

Name	Phone	Location	Island
Flying Cloud	(242) 394-5067	Paradise Island Ferry Terminal - 0.3 mi. (0.5 km) West-Southwest of Paradise Island	New Providence
Sandy Toes	(242) 363-8637	Rose Island	Rose Island
Sea Island Adventures	(242) 325-3910	3.1 mi. (5.0 km) West of Cable Beach	New Providence

If you are considering the option of chartering a boat, you can reserve one from the following firms:

CHARTER AND RENTAL SERVICES

Name	Phone	Location	Island
Bahama Boat Excursions	(242) 421-0071	0.3 mi. (0.5 km) West-Southwest of Paradise Island	New Providence

Docking

The largest resort on the island, Atlantis Harborside Resort, caters to sailors and even has one of the best yachting marinas in the area. Amenities include tie-up and dock assistance, single- and three-phase power, telephone service, 24-hour "room" service to each vessel, daily trash pick-up, laundry services, private catering services, vending machines, and transportation between the marina and the resort.

Is your plan to visit Paradise Island using your own boat, or a charter from another location? This next table provides a quick summary of marinas in the area.

MARINAS

Name	Phone	Location
Bayshore Marina	393-8233	0.3 mi. (0.5 km) West-Southwest of Paradise Island
Hurricane Hole Marina	(242) 363-	Marina Way - 3.5 mi. (5.6 km) North-Northeast

	3600		of Nassau
Marina Village Docks	(242)	327-6400	0.2 mi. (0.3 km) West of Paradise Island
Paradise Harbour Club Marina	(242)	363-2992	0.8 mi. (1.3 km) East of Paradise Island

With such a short amount of travel time between Florida and Paradise Island, it makes perfect sense why this is such a popular destination amongst yachts. Even if you don't sail yourself, there are a number of ways to get out on the open sea, and you should definitely make plans to do so during your stay.

Taxis on Paradise Island

Taxis are the main method of transportation on Paradise Island

Because of the all-inclusive nature of Paradise Island, many tourists choose to forgo renting a vehicle and instead choose to hire a taxi service when they are in need of transport to a place where they cannot walk or get a ride from their resort shuttle. Thankfully, taxis here are clean and known for their friendly customer service.

Taxi Companies

It isn't hard to find a taxi on Paradise Island. The drivers know that their best bet is to stick to hotels, beaches, restaurants, shopping areas, and other popular attractions, and so you'll almost always see a driver waiting to pick up a passenger in any of these locations.

Rates, Fares, and Fees

Rates for taxi services in the Bahamas are strictly put in place by the government, and your driver should have a list of how much it will take you to get from one place to another in his or her vehicle.

There are a few extra expenses to be aware of. First, to cross the bridge to Paradise Island it costs $1(USD) in toll fare. So, if you're catching a cab from the airport to your resort, or you'd like to spend some time in Nassau you'll need to be prepared to hand a dollar to the driver as you reach the toll. Next, each rider is welcome to store two small pieces of luggage in the trunk of the car. Anything over the two piece limit will cost an extra $2(USD). Finally, be aware that the prices listed above are based on a two passenger occupancy. If you're traveling with more people it will be another $3(USD) per person.

A great perk of the taxis on Paradise Island is that they can be hired by the hour as tour guides. You'll have to negotiate the price with your driver, but it usually comes out to being about $50 to $100(USD) per hour for up to five passengers.

Tipping your driver is definitely something you should do, but as it is in the United States, you should tip based upon the level of service you receive. The common price is 15 percent of your final bill, but you are free to tip more or less.

There is no need to go out of your way to rent a car when there are so many taxis on Paradise Island just waiting to pick you up and show you around. Add in the fact that the prices are relatively inexpensive and the drivers are known for their hospitality, and you know you'll be making the right choice when you decide to make taxis your get-around go-to.

Nassau Transportation Options

Head to Nassau, where you shouldn't have any trouble making your way around time

The capital, and busiest city, in the Bahamas is Nassau. Set on New Providence, Nassau welcomes tourists from all around the world with interests of all sorts from shopping to fishing, and everyone can happily find hours of activities to keep them occupied. Because of its popularity, getting to Nassau isn't difficult, and once you've arrived there are numerous options available for getting around.

Getting There

Most tourists find that the easiest method of getting to Nassau is to fly due to the fact that the international airport is located right in town. Sailing is a great option, even for those who are not as well-versed in the intricacies of the sport because of the island nation's close proximity to Florida, and cruising is another popular option.

Getting Around

Getting around Nassau isn't a difficult feat. Many tourists arrive prepared to walk and hail a cab at times when the trip is too long to make the trek on foot, though renting a car is certainly an option if an expensive one. Buses are available as well, and if you'd like to spend some time exploring the other islands in the chain, ferries will be of great use to you.

Air Travel

The major international airport that connects Bahamas with the outside world is located just eight miles outside of Nassau. This means that quick, direct flights with no layovers are a very real possibility for tourists flying directly to the Bahamas from another international hub. As you book your flight, be on the lookout for flights with major commercial airlines such as Delta Airlines, Jet Blue, Air Canada, and British Airways, among many others.

The complete list of airlines that fly to the Bahamas, as well as everything you need to know about air travel for this type of vacation can be found when you read on Air Travel page in this book.

Sailing

Just a short hop away from the United States, Nassau is a common destination for sailors, especially due to its international fame. However, sailors coming into Nassau should realize that this city can get very crowded, especially when three or more cruise ships are docked. Speaking of cruise ships, while you will unlikely be sharing lanes with them very often, it is easy to get a little tense when they are nearby. So while sailing your own vessel can be cheaper than airfare or a cruise, there are a few downsides too.

Cruising

The Prince George Wharf, which is located in downtown Nassau, is a major Port of Call for many popular cruise lines. Carnival, Celebrity, Princess, Disney, and more major lines are constantly sailing in and out of the wharf, allowing passengers to get off and explore this very popular destination.

Rental Cars

The amount you'll spend renting a car will depend on the type of car you choose to rent, the amenities you request, and the time of year you visit. Taking all this into account, the amount you spend will vary greatly, yet most agree the price is still more than what is necessary given the public transportation options available in the area. Plenty of tourists still decide to go the rental route, a great choice for those planning to spend a lot of time exploring, those traveling in large groups, and those with physical handicaps.

Taxis

Taxis are a great form of transportation and one of the most commonly used ones by tourists staying in Nassau. Because this area is so heavy with tourist traffic, you'll hardly find it difficult to find a driver to take you around, no matter where you are. The one thing you'll need to pay attention to is pricing. In the Bahamas there are two different ways that pricing is handled. Some drivers have meters, charging a set $3 and an additional $0.40 per quarter mile. Others charge set rates that have been put in place by the government, so you will have to ask your driver up front how much your fare will be at the end. Despite the possible difficulty figuring out the pricing, the drivers are known to be friendly and bad cab service is rarely reported.

Buses

If you ask for information about taking the bus in Nassau, you may get a funny look. This is because buses in the Bahamas are actually called jitneys. They run every day from 6:30 a.m. to 7:00 p.m., and at $1.50(USD) per person each way, they are without a doubt the cheapest way to get around. Jitneys spend their days making the rounds to all of the most popular tourist attractions, restaurants, resorts, beaches, and shopping centers, so it shouldn't be too hard to find a jitney that will get you near to your destination.

Ferries

Ferries are a very important part of inter-island transportation in the Bahamas. If you plan to spend your days in the country visiting as many islands as you can, using one of the many ferry services will be the most scenic and affordable option available to you. However, if your travels will keep you on New Providence Island this time around, the only ferry you need to worry about is the one that goes back and forth between Nassau and Paradise Island all day.

A vacation in Nassau is a once-in-a-lifetime opportunity for most tourists, and many spend months and even years planning every detail of their trip. Fortunately, transportation arrangements are easily decided upon and made, so you can focus on other aspects of your getaway.

Nassau by Airplane

How to Reach Nassau by Airplane?

Nassau is home to the largest and busiest airport in the Bahamas

Located just outside of Nassau is the main international airport that supplies all foreign visitors to the Bahamas. This is great news for tourists who plan to make Nassau the location of their next vacation, because it allows for the possibility of a direct flight with no layovers.

The Lynden Pindling International Airport is the largest in the island chain, and all international air travel first stops here before tourists can make connecting flights to other, less populous, islands. Although tourists from around the world make the journey every day, 80 percent of tourism comes from the United States perhaps because of its close proximity; a flight from Florida takes less than one hour. One of the bonuses of returning to the United States from the Bahamas is that it is a US Pre-Clearance Facility, which means that tourists can go through Customs and Immigration in the Bahamas and not have to do it again when they arrive in the United States.

Private Planes

If you're skilled in flying your own plane, the Bahamas is the perfect destination for you because they have no issue allowing private planes to fly into the island. Most flights will originate in Florida where they can fuel up and make the less than one hour flight to Nassau.

First on your to-do list if you're flying into the Bahamas is to file and International Flight Plan and activate it on Miami's radio frequencies 122.2, 122.4, or 126.7. As you near the Bahamas, you'll switch over to Nassau radio frequencies 124.2 or 128.0 to close out your flight plan. When you arrive, ever passenger on board will be asked to present three copies of the C7A Bahamas Customs form, a Bahamas Immigration Card, and proof of citizenship.

Keep the following factors in mind as you plan your flight to the islands:

➢ Each passenger on board is required to have their own Coast Guard approved life jacket.

➢ Although private airports have the right to charge what they wish, private planes that weight under 6,000 pounds will not be charged landing or tie down fees when they land at government airports.

➢ Overtime Customs and Immigration fees are waived as well if the passengers are traveling for recreational purposes.

➢ Lighted runways are available at Lynden Pindling International Airport and the Freeport Airport so night landings are allowed. All other arrivals and departures must take place during daylight hours.

> ➢ Fuel is not available on every island, but you'll never be more than 20 minutes away from fuel by air.

Your flight back to the United States will require you to complete a Gen Dec and turn in a copy of your Immigration Card. You will first file your International Flight Plan at 800-WXBRIEF and activate your flight with the Nassau radio frequencies listed above. As you fly, listen to VOR 116.7. Before you touch down in Miami, you'll receive a discrete transponder code from FDD 126.7 Miami Radio, and you will continue on that radio station as you close out your flight.

Questions regarding private flights to the Bahamas can be made o the Aviation Specialist at the Bahamas Ministry of Tourism, who can be contacted at 800-32-SPORT.

This table informs you of which airlines are flying non-stop from the U.S. as well as which airports they fly from. Not all of the options you will be shown on the web make sense so it's useful to see which airlines provide direct service to this location.

LYNDEN PINDLING INTERNATIONAL AIRPORT U.S. FLIGHTS		
To/From	Airport Code	Airlines
Baltimore, MD, USA	BWI	AirTran, US Airways
Detroit, MI, USA	DTW	KLM, US Airways

Fort Lauderdale, FL, USA	FLL	Bahamasair, Jet Blue, SkyBahamas
Manchester, NH, USA	MHT	US Airways
Miami, FL, USA	MIA	American Eagle, Bahamasair
New Orleans, LA, USA	MSY	US Airways
Orlando, FL, USA	MCO	Bahamasair, Jet Blue
St. Louis, MO, USA	STL	US Airways
West Palm Beach, FL, USA	PBI	Bahamasair
Windsor Locks, CT, USA	BDL	US Airways

The following table displays airlines that have direct flights from locations in Canada.

LYNDEN PINDLING INTERNATIONAL AIRPORT CANADIAN FLIGHTS		
To/From	Airport Code	Airlines
Montreal, Canada	YUL	Air Canada

Flying to Nassau from the Caribbean

Not everyone flies into Nassau and stays there for their whole vacation. Island-hopping is a very popular pursuit, and tourists have the option of booking a domestic flight with BahamasAir which offers daily flights to 14 other islands and even a few flights from the United States.

Another option if you plan on visiting another island is to charter a private flight with a Fixed-Base Operator (FBO) to fly into one of the 60 or so other airports or air strips throughout the Bahamas. The chart that follows offers contact information for some of the better known charter companies leaving from LPIA.

See the following chart for scheduled air service from other Caribbean airports. If you can't get a flight directly from an airport near you, connecting through another Caribbean airport might prove to be a very good solution.

LYNDEN PINDLING INTERNATIONAL AIRPORT CARIBBEAN FLIGHTS		
To/From	Airport Code	Airlines
Abaco, Bahamas	MHH	Abaco Air, Bahamasair, SkyBahamas, Western Air
Abaco, Bahamas	TCB	Bahamasair
Acklins, Bahamas	AXP	Bahamasair
Acklins, Bahamas	CRI	Bahamasair
Andros, Bahamas	COX	Performance Air, Western Air

Andros, Bahamas	MAY	Flamingo Air, Performance Air
Andros, Bahamas	SAQ	Western Air
Cat Island, Bahamas	ATC	SkyBahamas
Cat Island, Bahamas	CAT	SkyBahamas
Eleuthera, Bahamas	ELH	Bahamasair, SkyBahamas
Eleuthera, Bahamas	GHB	Bahamasair
Freeport, Grand Bahama Island	FPO	Bahamasair, SkyBahamas, Western Air
Georgetown, Grand Cayman	GCM	British Airways
Great Exuma, Bahamas	GGT	Bahamasair, SkyBahamas
Havana, Cuba	HAV	Bahamasair
Inagua, Bahamas	IGA	Bahamasair
Kingston, Jamaica	KTP	Caribbean Airlines
Long Island, Bahamas	LGI	Bahamasair, SkyBahamas
Long Island, Bahamas	SML	Bahamasair, SkyBahamas
Mayaguana, Bahamas	MYG	Bahamasair
Normans Cay, Bahamas	NMC	Performance Air
Providenciales, Turks and Caicos Islands	PLS	Bahamasair, British Airways, Intercaribbean Airways
Rock Sound, Eleuthera	RSD	Bahamasair

San Salvador, Bahamas	ZSA	Bahamasair, SkyBahamas
Staniel Cay, Bahamas	TYM	Flamingo Air, Performance Air
the Bahamas	MYE3	Flamingo Air
the Bahamas	MYEB	Flamingo Air
the Berry Islands, Bahamas	GHC	SkyBahamas
the Bimini Islands, Bahamas	BIM	SkyBahamas, Western Air

Getting to Nassau

After arriving at the airport, the trip to your accommodations in Nassau is a quick one. You can rent a car directly from the airport, or you can have a taxi take you. Taxis can be a bit confusing, because some operate on meters while others will charge you one set rate. Just make sure to confirm that method your driver uses before you take off, and you should be fine. If you get into a cab that offers set rates, you'll pay $27(USD) for two passengers, plus $3(USD) for each additional passenger to get to Nassau from the airport, plus $2(USD) per piece of luggage stored in the trunk after the first two free pieces, and tip.

Flight is the quickest way to get to Nassau from around the world, and as such the most popular. Book your flight early to ensure you'll be able to fly when you want and that you find the best deals.

Use the following chart to find out how to call an air charter firms serving this region.

CHARTER OPERATORS

Name	Phone	Location
Bahama Hoppers at MYNN	(242) 335-1650	Odyssey Aviation at NAS - 4.3 mi. (7.0 km) South West of Cable Beach
Flamingo Air at NAS	(242) 351-4963	Lynden Pindling International Airport - 4.1 mi. (6.6 km) South West of Cable Beach
Golden Wings Charter	(242) 377-0039	Lynden Pindling International Airport - 4.1 mi. (6.6 km) South West of Cable Beach
Intercaribbean Airways at NAS	(855) 244-7940	Lynden Pindling International Airport - 4.1 mi. (6.6 km) South West of Cable Beach
LeAir Charter Main Office	(242) 377-2356	Lynden Pindling International Airport - 4.1 mi. (6.6 km) South West of Cable Beach
Monarch Air Group at NAS	(242) 702-0200	Lynden Pindling International Airport - 4.1 mi. (6.6 km) South West of Cable Beach
Novah Flight Services	322-7677	Nassau
Performance Air	(242) 341-	30 Cowpen Road - Nassau

Charters	3281	
Seabird Air in Nassau	(242) 362-1224	Nassau
Southern Air Charter	(242) 323-7217	Lynden Pindling International Airport - 4.1 mi. (6.6 km) South West of Cable Beach

Ferries to Nassau

Add a little adventure to your Nassau vacation with a ferry ride to another island

Numerous ferry services make the rounds on a daily basis throughout the Bahamas. If you're planning on doing some island hopping and spending some time outside of Nassau, you'll want to become acquainted with each option so you can determine which is optimal for your needs. The ferries can be sorted into four broad categories, and knowing a bit about each of them gives you a better idea of which service to book with.

Mail Boats

Once upon a time, Mail Boats were the premier way to get around the Bahamas. Today, they remain the least expensive option for getting to such a wide variety of islands. What you need to know about Mail

Boats is that they are government run venture primarily used to haul transport. Locals got the idea to start hopping on board to visit other islands, and soon the vessels had been redesigned to carry passengers as well as freight.

The biggest complaint that tourists have is that the Mail Boats move slowly. You'll have the best luck if you use this service to travel between two islands that are located nearby one another. Mail Boats originate in Potter's Cay, which is less than 10 minutes from the center of Nassau, and sail to the Abacos, Acklins, Andros, the Berry Islands, Bimini, Cat Island, Eleuthera, the Exumas, Grand Bahama, Harbour Island, Inagua, Long Island, Mayaguana, and San Salvador,.

More information about this particular ferry service can be learned by contacting the Dockmaster's Offic at 242-393-1064.

Fast Ferries

Also originating from Potter's Cay is the Bahamas Fast Ferry Service, a much quicker alternative to the slow-going Mail Boats. In fact, Fast Ferries were created with the specific intent of providing quicker service than Mail Boats. This service connects Abaco, Andros, Eleuthera, the Exumas, and Nassau.

Every day the Fast Ferries leave from Potter's Cay at 8:00 a.m., transport passengers to the other islands, and returns again at 6:00 p.m.

Albury's Ferries

Those who plan to take a day or two to explore the Marsh Harbour Island will want to take advantage Albury's Ferries. Albury's has been servicing the Bahamas for nearly 50 years, and with a fleet of 12 fiberglass boats provides transportation between Marsh Harbour, Man-of-War, Hope Town, Guana, and Scotland on a daily basis.

International Ferries

If you're traveling to the Bahamas from the state of Florida, you may consider making the two-and-a-half hour trip aboard the Pinar del Rio ferry, also known as the Bahamas Express Ferry, to Grand Bahama Island. From there, you can transfer to Nassau aboard a plan between the Grand Bahama International Airport and the Lynden Pindling International Airport.

Pinar del Rio leaves Ft. Lauderdale, Florida at 10:00 a.m. Every day of the week except for Wednesdays, and returns that evening at 7:30 p.m. This makes it easy to plan a quick day trip to the island, especially since it is just $49.50(USD) for a one way trip.

Another ferry service from Florida is the Maverick, which operates out of Miami on the weekend. Also for $49.50(USD), you can leave from the Port of Miami at 9:00 a.m. and sail to Alice Town on North Bimini, where you'll arrive around noon and stay until 5:00 p.m.

It is also important to note that there are several smaller ferry services around the islands that serve the purpose of offering transportation between two specific places. One great example of this is the Paradise Island Ferry right on New Providence Island. This ferry costs $3(USD) each way and brings tourists between the center of Nassau to Paradise Island in under 20 minutes. This ferry does not run on a set schedule; instead it continues to travel back and forth between the two islands throughout the day. Another example is the ferry that travels between Treasure Cay and Green Turtle Cay each day.

The numerous ferry options can be tricky to figure out, but once you do a world of day trip opportunities open up to you, making your Nassau getaway all the more magical.

FERRY ROUTES, NASSAU				
Location Served	Dock A	Dock B	Company	Frequency
Abaco	Bahamas Ferries Potters Cay Dock	Sandy Point Ferry Terminal	Bahamas Ferries	1 to 2 days per week

Acklins	Bahamas Ferries Potters Cay Dock	Acklins Ferry Dock	The Mail Boat Company	None
Andros	Bahamas Ferries Potters Cay Dock	Fresh Creek Ferry Terminal	Bahamas Ferries	1 to 2 days per week
Eleuthera	Bahamas Ferries Potters Cay Dock	Current Island Ferry Dock	Bahamas Ferries	1 to 2 days per week
Eleuthera	Bahamas Ferries Potters Cay Dock	Harbour Island Ferry Dock	Bahamas Ferries	1 to 2 days per week
Eleuthera	Bahamas Ferries Potters Cay Dock	Spanish Wells Ferry Dock	Bahamas Ferries	1 to 2 days per week
Grand Bahama	Bahamas Ferries Potters Cay Dock	Freeport Harbour Terminal One	Bahamas Ferries	1 to 2 days per week
Great Exuma	Bahamas Ferries Potters Cay Dock	Government Docks	Bahamas Ferries	1 to 2 days per week
Harbour Island	Bahamas Ferries Potters Cay Dock	Harbour Island Ferry Terminal	Bahamas Ferries	1 to 2 days per week
Long Island	Bahamas Ferries Potters Cay Dock	Long Island Ferry Dock	Bahamas Ferries	1 to 2 days per week
the Berry Islands	Bahamas Ferries Potters Cay Dock	Great Harbour Cay Fery Dock	The Mail Boat Company	None

Nassau Rental Cars

If you plan to explore outside of Nassau city limits, a rental car might just work for you

Nassau has been built up in such a manner that tourists who plan to stay in town will have no need for a rental car. Hotel and casino shuttles, buses, and taxis can get you everywhere you can't walk with little trouble. Still, some people feel more comfortable with a car at their disposal, others need to have a car on hand perhaps for medical purposes, and those who plan to explore other parts of the island will find renting a car to be the least expensive option for them.

Renting a Car

You can expect that you'll need to be at least 21-years-old, but more often 25, plus have a valid driver's license from your country of origin. This will allow you to drive in the Bahamas for up to three months. If you plan to stay longer, make sure you order an International Driver's License (IDL) before your trip. With these facts in mind, you're ready to choose which agency to rent with.

Both large, international franchises and locally owned independent rental agencies exist in Nassau. Local agencies typically offer the better deals and more personalized service because their business relies on word-of-mouth, but international chains tend to give visitors a sense of security because they are renting with a name they know and probably trust. Ask around if you know anyone who has visited

Nassau in the past and you may get a first hand recommendation that will help you to make the final call.

Check out the following table for many of the rental agencies serving Nassau.

VEHICLE RENTAL COMPANIES		
Name	Phone	Location
Ace Auto Rental	(242) 676-7376	East Bay Street - Nassau
Adrana's Car Rental	324-9257	Springfield Road - Nassau
Avis Downtown Nassau	326-6380	1 Cumberland St - Downtown Nassau
Centreville Car Rentals Co Ltd	326-8270	East Ave Centreville - Nassau
Driver Rent-A-Car & Sales	394-8551	East Bay Street - Nassau
Newbold Rent A Car	(242) 328-0500	97 Saint Charles Vincent - Nassau
O & B's Car Rentals	323-2581	Thompson Blvd - Nassau
Virgo Car Rental	393-8250	20B Airport Industrial Park - Nassau

Driving in Nassau

Driving in Nassau is not terribly difficult as long as you keep one rule in mind: stay on the left side of the road. This is the opposite of what drivers from the United States are used to, but with a little practice it can quickly become second nature. Roads can be narrow, which can cause some difficulty, but nothing that you cannot overcome as an experienced driver.

Try to stay off the road during rush hour, when traffic can become heavy with locals weaving in and out of traffic, practicing their aggressive driving styles. Always wear a seat belt, keep children in the appropriate safety seats, and drive defensively. It also helps to have a GPS or map on hand to help you get around.

The Cost of Renting a Car

The cost to rent a car in Nassau will depend on the type of car you choose as well as the amenities you request, the time of year you rent (the off-season brings greater discounts), and where you rent from. Local agencies are known for having better prices, but also rent out older model vehicles, so you may be driving around a clunker. With all of that in mind, you can still expect to spend anywhere from $80 to $120(USD) a day, plus the cost of insurance if you choose to purchase it.

Gas Stations

Even though you should not have any problems locating places to refuel, you still may want to check out the table below for an idea where some of them are located.

GAS STATIONS

Name	Location
Esso On The Run	1.0 mi. (1.6 km) South of Nassau
Esso Service Station	3.2 mi. (5.2 km) Northeast of Nassau
Esso Soldier Road	Soldier Road - 0.3 mi. (0.5 km) North-Northeast of Nassau
Esso Wulff and Mackey	Wulff Road and Mackey Street - 2.0 mi. (3.2 km) Northeast of Nassau
Gas Station Balfour Avenue	Balfour Avenue - 1.3 mi. (2.1 km) North of Nassau
Gas Station Carter Street	Carter Street - 2.2 mi. (3.6 km) North-Northwest of Nassau
Gas Station East West Highway	East West Highway - 0.9 mi. (1.4 km) North of Nassau
Gas Station Harrold Road	Harrold Road - 0.8 mi. (1.3 km) Northwest of Nassau
Gas Station Mackey and Madeira	Mackey Street and Madeira Street - 2.5 mi. (4.0 km) North-Northeast of Nassau
Gas Station Madeira and Montrose	Madeira Street and Montrose Avenue - 2.4 mi. (3.8 km) North-Northeast of Nassau
Gas Station Montrose and Rosetta	Rosetta Street and Montrose Avenue - 2.5 mi. (4.1 km) North-Northeast of Nassau
Gas Station Poinciana Avenue	Poinciana Avenue - 1.4 mi. (2.3 km) North of Nassau
Gas Station Portago and Thompson	Portago and Thompson Boulevard - 2.1 mi. (3.3 km) Northwest of Nassau
Gas Station Queen Sports	Thompson Boulevard - 1.9 mi. (3.1 km) North-Northwest

Center	of Nassau
Gas Station Robinson and Baillou Hill Roads	Robinson and Baillou Hill Roads - 1.0 mi. (1.7 km) North-Northwest of Nassau
Gas Station Robinson and Old Trail	Old Trail and Robinson Roads - 1.5 mi. (2.4 km) Northeast of Nassau
Gas Station Sears Road	Sears Road - 2.6 mi. (4.2 km) North-Northwest of Nassau
Gas Station Shirley Street and John Evans	Shirley Street and John Evans Road - 3.2 mi. (5.1 km) Northeast of Nassau
Gas Station Shirley and Albury	Shirley Street and Albury Lane - 3.0 mi. (4.8 km) North-Northeast of Nassau
Gas Station Wulff and Minnie	Wulff Road and Minnie Street - 1.8 mi. (2.9 km) North-Northeast of Nassau
Gas Station Wulff and Montrose	Wulff Road and Montrose Avenue - 1.9 mi. (3.0 km) North-Northeast of Nassau
Gas Station Wulff and Soldier Roads	Wulff and Soldier Roads - 2.4 mi. (3.8 km) Northeast of Nassau
Gibson & Delancy Gas	Miami Street - Nassau
On the Run	Farrington Road and Thompson Boulevard - 2.6 mi. (4.2 km) Northwest of Nassau
Shell	2.4 mi. (3.8 km) East of Cable Beach
Shell Marathon Road	Marathon Road - 2.1 mi. (3.3 km) Northeast of Nassau
Texaco	3.5 mi. (5.6 km) North-Northwest of Nassau

Texaco	3.1 mi. (4.9 km) North of Nassau
Texaco Baillou Hill Road	Baillou Hill Road - 0.9 mi. (1.4 km) North-Northwest of Nassau
Texaco Soldier Road	Soldier Road - 0.3 mi. (0.5 km) North of Nassau

Two of the main downsides to driving in Nassau are that parking is hard to come by and gas is expensive. Be prepared to drive in circles looking for a spot to open up, or to park a good distance out from your destination and walk, and have enough money on hand to pay more than $4(USD) a gallon on gas

Sailing and Boating Near Nassau

Known for plenty of other things, Nassau still has a pretty sizable sailing scene too

Among its many attributes, Nassau is a prime sailing destination within the Bahamas. Not only can you make your way to this port internationally, but you can also fly to the island and participate in a sail around the islands for some sightseeing or as part of a fishing, snorkeling, or diving excursion.

It takes only about eight hours to sail between Miami, Florida and Nassau, which is probably why the area sees so much traffic amongst

American yachters. Even if you don't plan to stay for your entire trip in Nassau, the town is known for having the best provisioning in the Bahamas (despite the high cost), so many sailors will stop here as their first port of entry, stay for a few nights, and then move on to the other islands.

If you're simply wanting to experience some time on the open water, without the stress and cost involved with renting a boat you should take a day sailing excursion. Take a look at the table that follows to get contact information for area day sail providers.

BOAT EXCURSIONS		
Name	Phone	Location
Barefoot Sailing Cruises	(242) 393-0820	3.1 mi. (5.0 km) North of Nassau
Party Cat Cruises	(954) 727-5339	East Bay Street - 3.4 mi. (5.5 km) Northeast of Nassau
Seaworld Explorer	(242) 356-2548	Downtown Nassau
Stuart's Cove's Snorkel Bahamas	(800) 879-9832	Stuart's Cove's Snorkel Bahamas - Downtown Nassau
Sunshine Cruises	(242) 327-5122	Woodes Rogers Walk - Downtown Nassau

If you're serious about a boat charter, you can contact one of these companies:

CHARTER AND RENTAL SERVICES		
Name	Phone	Location
Amarok Sailing Charters	(242) 477-4471	Nassau Yacht Haven - 0.5 mi. (0.8 km) South of Paradise Island
Watersports Cruise Total Package	393-0998	Bishop Street - Nassau

Docking

Every marina on New Providence Island is considered an official port-of-entry, so you can decide which marina you'd like to dock your yacht at in advance and sail there directly.

Considering the option of sailing to Nassau using your own vessel, or a boat you charter elsewhere? This next chart lists potential docking spots.

MARINAS		
Name	Phone	Location
East Bay Yacht Club	(242) 394-1816	3.2 mi. (5.1 km) North-Northeast of Nassau
Elizabeth on the Bay Marina	(242) 424-7374	Downtown Nassau

Harbour Central Marina	323-2172	671 Bay Street - Nassau
Harbour Club Marina	(242) 393-0771	3.4 mi. (5.5 km) Northeast of Nassau
Harbour View Marina	394-7085	East Bay Street - Nassau
Marlin Marine	(242) 393-7873	3.3 mi. (5.3 km) Northeast of Nassau
Nassau Yacht Club	(242) 393-5132	3.6 mi. (5.7 km) Northeast of Nassau
Nassau Yacht Haven	(242) 393-8173	3.3 mi. (5.3 km) North-Northeast of Nassau
Olde Towne Marina	(242) 327-6533	West Bay Street - Nassau

As you sail into port, fly your yellow quarantine flag so that customs will know that you have not yet been cleared. When you pull in, you will be asked to present proof of citizenship, a passport, and another form of photo identification for each passenger on board, then you will be required to fill out an immigration card. Finally, you'll pay between $150 and $300(USD) depending upon the length of your boat. This fee covers the cost of your cruising permit, fishing permit, and departure tax, and is good for up to four people. If you have more passengers on board, you will see additional charges.

After obtaining your permit, you are free to sail around the islands. Once you find a slip to dock your boat at, make sure to keep your belongings locked up at all times, as petty crime against yachters in the area is on the rise. If you have any questions about sailing to Nassau, contact the Port Authority Department at 242-322-1596 or 242-326-7354.

Knowing which options are available to you, you're better prepared to decide how you want to get out to sea when you visit Nassau. Will you sail yourself from south Florida or wait until you get to town and participate in a tour? The choice is your and you can't make a wrong decision.

Nassau Taxis

Taxis are plentiful in Nassau

Tourists from around the world flock to Nassau on a regular basis and it is without question the busiest town in the Bahamas. This lends itself to being one of the most traffic-riddled towns in the island chain, a fact which can turn many foreigners away from wanting to drive themselves around. Fortunately, Nassau is set up so that tourists never have to want for a rental car because taxis are so easily available.

Taxi Companies

You'll find taxis milling around anywhere with a high tourist turn out: Prince George Wharf, Lynden Pindling International Airport, as well as hotels, restaurants, shopping centers, and beaches.

Be sure to look at this chart to help you reach a local cab company if you are wanting a taxi.

TAXI SERVICES		
Name	Phone	Location
Bahamas Taxi Cab Union	(242) 323-7900	Nassau
Meter Cab Taxi Service	(242) 323-5111	Davis St - Nassau
Taxicab Service	(242) 323-4323	Nassau
The Jolly Green Giant Taxi Service	(242) 394-8294	Nassau

Rates, Fares, and Fees

The one turn off about taxis in Nassau is that determining the cost of your trip can be a bit confusing. Some drivers use meters while others offer rates set by the government. You will always want to ask your driver how he or she determines the fare before you start driving.

If you're in a metered vehicle, you will pay $3 as a base fare, then an additional $0.40(USD) for each quarter mile traveled. Set rates are created with departure and arrival points in mind.

In addition for the cost of your trip, you will also pay an extra $3(USD) for each passenger if you're riding with more than two. You're allowed to store two small pieces of luggage in the trunk per person, but any pieces beyond that will incur an extra fee of $2(USD) per bag. Finally, if you decide you want to venture out of Nassau and see what's what over on Paradise Island, you will be responsible for paying the $1(USD) toll that is charged to cross the bridge.

If you'd like to take a tour of the island, consider hiring your taxi driver by the hour to take you around. It will cost you between $50 n $100 an hour for five passengers depending upon what you've negotiated, but the local tales and viewpoints are worth the charge.

Taxi drivers in Nassau depend on their tips. If you've received good service, do not hesitate to offer a gratuity of 15 percent or more.

Now that you have an idea of what to expect when you hire a taxi in Nassau, you're ready to move towards your final decision regarding whether or not you'll rent a car. Most seasoned Nassau visitors will tell you it isn't a necessity, only something to do if it makes you feel comfortable.

Weather
Learn About the Weather of the Bahamas

The weather of the Bahamas offers travelers warm sun and cooling winds

The weather in the Bahamas is a treat for travelers. Although the chain is made up of over 700 low-lying islands stretching from just east of Florida down into the Caribbean, most of the islands have very similar climates.

The Bahamas temperatures are moderated by the warm waters of the Gulf Stream. Additionally, because the Bahamas are closer to continental North America - and thus more easily effected by North American cold air systems - they are slightly cooler than other Caribbean islands.

Average temperatures in the Bahamas range from 80 to 90 degrees Fahrenheit (27 to 32 degrees Celsius) in the summer to 70 to 80 degrees Fahrenheit (21 to 27 degrees Celsius) in the winter. The northern Bahamian islands can be even a little cooler. Winds across the Bahamas keep vacations cool in the daytime and help lower the temperatures at night. Relative humidity is about 65% throughout the year, making temperatures feel a little warmer than they read at times.

The islands rainy season lasts from May to October, dropping an average of 4.3 inches of rain each month. October sees the heaviest amount, with approximately 8.10 inches, and June comes in at a close second with an average of 8.9 inches of rain. Still the Bahamas experiences about 310 days of sunshine each year, and averages 8 hours per day.

Although the Bahamas is located in the hurricane belt that lies across most of the Caribbean, many storms bypass the island chain and instead circle below it before heading north toward the United States. Of course, the islands are equipped to respond to a storm if one does hit.

Modern technology offers some reassurance to travelers who want to visit the Caribbean during the hurricane season, which lasts from June to November. Because hurricanes can be tracked from the time they form, travelers should have no problem preparing and canceling travel plans if necessary.

The table below contains selected climatological data for the Bahamas as reported at Nassau International Airport. While some islands are dryer than others, the climate throughout the Bahamas is fairly uniform; this table should give you a good idea of what the weather will be like in a given month, and what trends to expect during your vacation.

Month	Average Daily	Average Daily	Average Monthly	% Days with

Nassau & Paradise Island, The Bahamas

	High Temperature	Low Temperature	Precipitation	Rain
January	77.00°F	64.30°F	1.59 in	24.8%
February	77.10°F	64.70°F	1.61 in	26.2%
March	79.00°F	66.30°F	1.55 in	23.2%
April	80.90°F	68.50°F	2.26 in	19.7%
May	84.00°F	72.20°F	4.97 in	32.5%
June	87.10°F	75.60°F	7.01 in	43.2%
July	89.00°F	77.00°F	6.00 in	44.8%
August	89.20°F	77.10°F	6.46 in	50.3%
September	88.30°F	76.20°F	7.21 in	55.1%
October	85.20°F	74.00°F	6.56 in	35.6%
November	81.90°F	70.90°F	2.63 in	25.8%
December	78.30°F	66.40°F	1.59 in	24.1%

All in all, the weather in the Bahamas offers travelers cooling winds and warm temperatures to enjoy nearly every day of their journey.